Brendan & Erc in Exile
Volume 3

THE WEAPONS OF WAR

Imprimi Potest: ✠ Right Reverend William J. Driscoll, M.M.A.
Abbot of Most Holy Trinity Monastery

Nihil Obstat: Reverend Robert E. Nortz, M.M.A., S.T.L.
Censor Deputatus

Imprimatur: ✠ The Most Reverend Gregory J. Mansour, S.T.L.
Bishop of the Eparchy of Saint Maron of Brooklyn
18 July, 2019

The *Nihil Obstat* and *Imprimatur* are official declarations that a book or pamphlet is free of doctrinal or moral error. No implication is contained therein that those who have granted the *Nihil Obstat* or *Imprimatur* agree with the contents, opinions, or statements expressed.

www.maronitemonks.org

Published by Catholic Answers, Inc.
2020 Gillespie Way
El Cajon, California 92020
1-888-291-8000 orders
619-387-0042 fax
catholic.com

Printed in the United States of America

ISBN 978-1-68357-125-4

Cover sacrament symbols: Background: The Eucharist, Top Right: Anointing (5 crosses for the 5 senses), Clockwise: Marriage (2 rings), Priesthood (cope and collar), Reconciliation (stole and key), Confirmation (fire of the Holy Spirit), Baptism (shell and 3 streams of water).

To Jesus Christ,
hidden in the
Blessed Sacrament:
My Lord and Savior,
my Friend and my Life.

And in memory of
Br. Augustine Martin, M.M.A.
(1958-2016)
Whose help and encouragement
with these books was
invaluable.

INTRODUCTION

Although we may not see it, there is a war raging around us every day, a spiritual war that everyone who comes into this world must fight sooner or later if he wishes to save his soul. For the "kingdom of heaven has suffered violence, and men of violence take it by force" (Matt 11:12). Fortunately, God, who desires our salvation far more than we do, gives us an arsenal of spiritual weapons to help us in our fight against the world, the flesh, and the devil.

Now, there are many spiritual helps and many good books about them. The purpose of this book is to give an overview of the seven sacraments—some of the most powerful "weapons" that Christ left his Church Militant. It continues where *The Big Picture* left off. Salvation history gives us an understanding of the origins of this battle and the hope and joy that Christ gave us by his victory over sin and death; now, the sacraments provide the means of participating in the life of Jesus Christ and making that victory our own.

The pages that follow treat first of all the goal of our spiritual life—union with God in heaven—then the means of achieving that goal through the sacraments as well as avoiding its loss through sin. It is not accidental that much of the book focuses on the Holy Eucharist. Aside from being the "source and summit of the Christian life" (CCC 1324) since it contains the very Christ from whom all the sacraments receive their power and toward whom they are directed, it is also at the heart of our Catholic faith, a faith that is very much in need of strengthening in these days. As the Servant of God Fr. John A. Hardon, S.J. (†2000) did not hesitate to declare over twenty years ago, "The seat of the crisis in the Roman Catholic Church is the widespread loss of faith in the Real Presence."

Saint Alphonsus Ligouri once wrote that "God wills us to be saved; but for our greater good, he wills us to be saved as conquerors. While, therefore, we remain here, we have to live in a continual warfare; and if we should be saved, we have to fight and conquer." It is tragic how few realize that there is a war being waged against our souls—a war with eternal consequences—and fewer still make regular use of the power of the sacraments to help them, particularly the sacraments of confession and Communion. It is my hope that this little story of the sacraments will encourage Catholics to appreciate what they have (and to make more fervent and frequent use of them!) and to help non-Catholics better understand what we believe.

THE WEAPONS OF WAR

CONTENTS

CITY OF OLYMPIA

MONS OLYMPUS

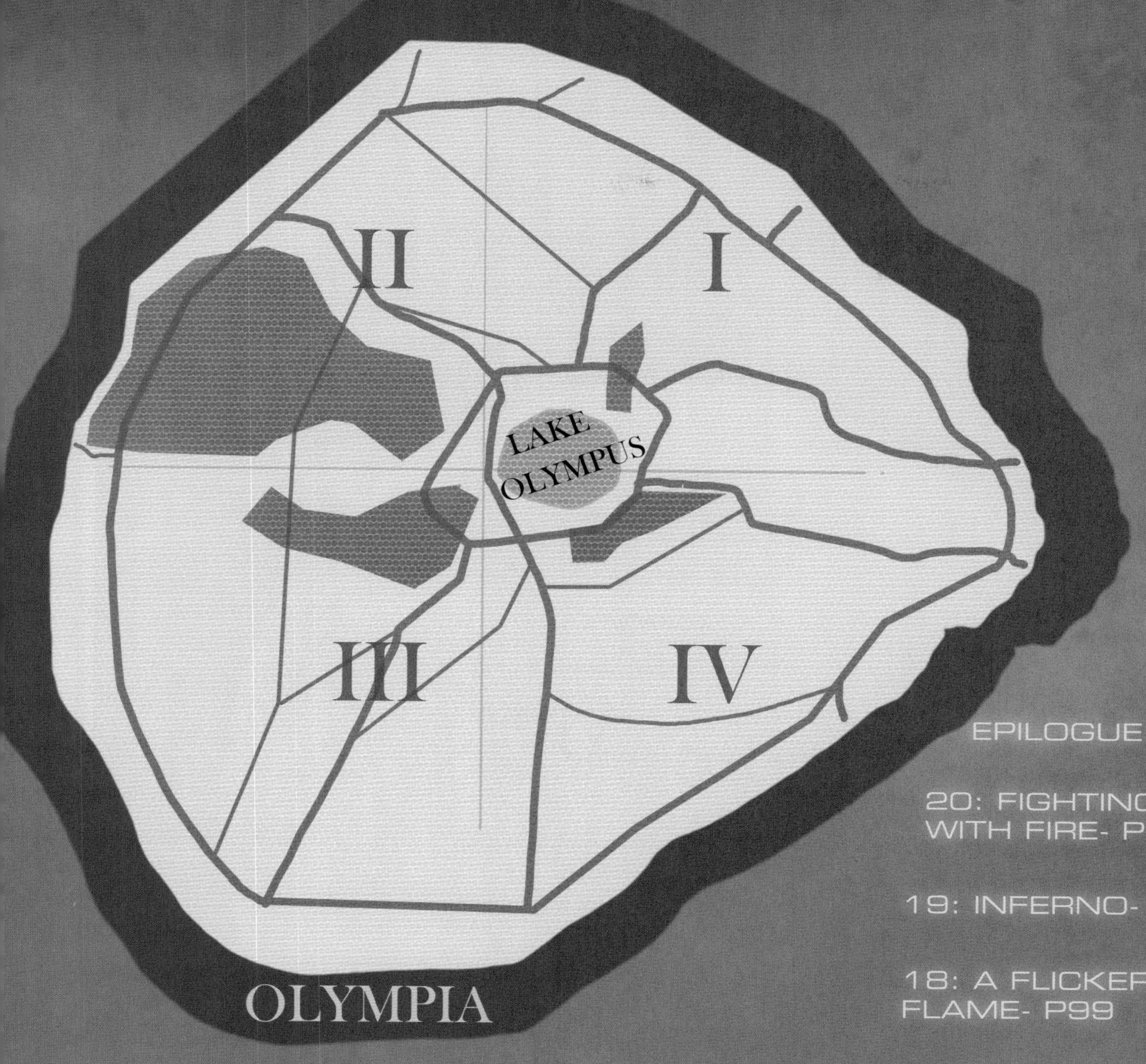

II

I

LAKE OLYMPUS

III

IV

OLYMPIA

LIA PLANUM

* FROM THE DOUAY-RHEIMS TRANSLATION.

Mars: Daedalia Planum region.

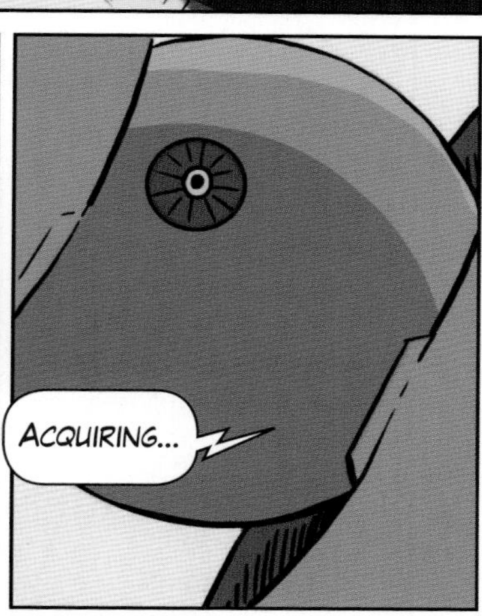

BZZT
WHAT JUST HAPPENED?!?
WE'VE LOST CONTACT WITH THE DRONE!
IT'S PROBABLY A DUD. JUST DROP THE SPARE...

ALL RIGHT. LAUNCHING SPARE...
THPPTT

I SURE HOPE THIS WORKS...

Meanwhile, on earth...
I baptize you...

In the name of the Father...

And of the Son...
I can't believe it...

And of the Holy Spirit.
After so much waiting and so many doubts...

The previous day...
I know baptism will change me...

But can I live up to it? I mean, as a son of God??

Not to worry! Nobody could live up to it without God's constant help!

Here. I was going to give you this tomorrow...

But it sounds like you need it more today!

A gift??
Just a small reminder of God's great love for you!

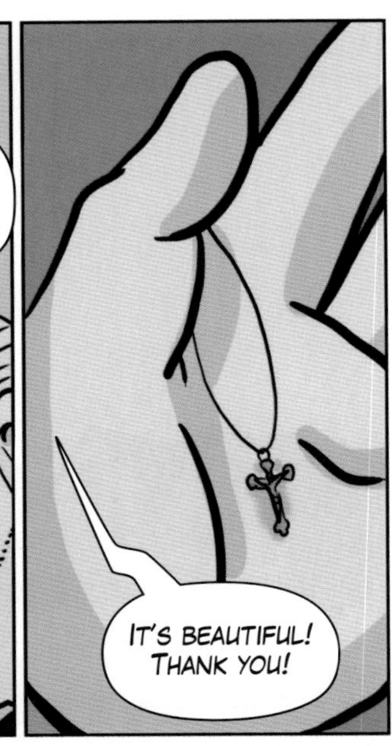
It's beautiful! Thank you!

Oof! Hmph!
Brendan, you have become a new creation and have clothed yourself in Christ...

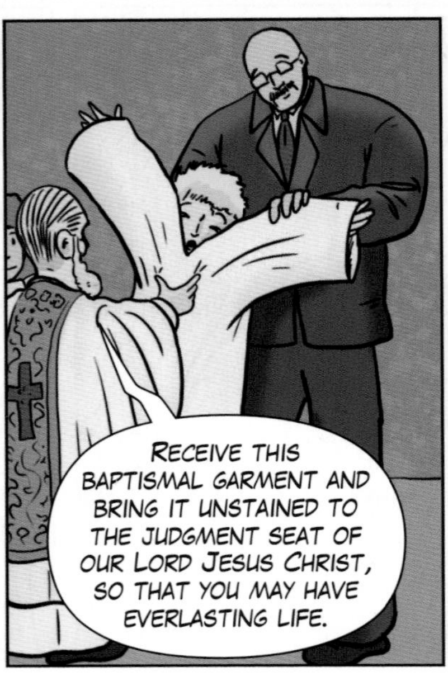
Receive this baptismal garment and bring it unstained to the judgment seat of our Lord Jesus Christ, so that you may have everlasting life.

You have been enlightened by Christ...

Walk always as a child of the light and keep the flame of faith alive in your heart...

Brendan, be sealed with the Gift of the Holy Spirit.
So many gifts!

The Body of Christ.
The Blood of Christ.
How can I thank you, my God?!

THE NEXT DAY...
CHAPTER 1
HEAVENLY HOPES
Welcome to
CG Industries
Cab & Carry
Space Port

CG

EXIT
TICKETS

Boarding

GOOD MORNING! HAVE YOU THOUGHT ABOUT GOD TODAY?

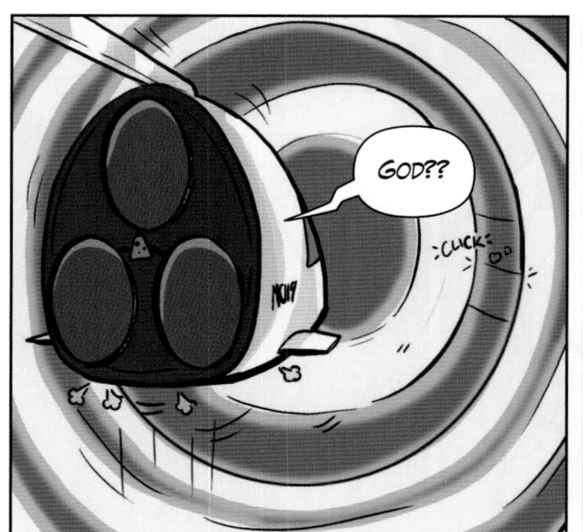
GOD??
CLICK

WHOOSH

SOON...
HOW CAN YOU NOT SEE HOW UNFAIR THAT IS??

WHAT'S UNFAIR?? IT'S GOD'S HOUSE... HE CAN INVITE WHOMEVER HE WANTS!

THAT'S FINE IF GOD WERE JUST A CELEBRITY THROWING A PARTY, BUT HE'S *GOD!!*
HE'S SUPPOSED TO BE *NICE* TO EVERYONE!

AND HE WOULDN'T BE IF HE DIDN'T LET EVERYONE INTO HEAVEN?
NO!

DIDN'T YOU JUST SAY THAT OUR DEEPEST DESIRE IS FOR HEAVEN?

AND THAT GOD PUT THAT DESIRE IN US?
YES...

SO HOW COULD HE NOT DELIVER ON HIS PROMISE?? HOW COULD GOD *LIE* TO US?!

AND IF THE DEVIL WANTED TO FIND HIS FULFILLMENT IN HEAVEN, SHOULD GOD LET *HIM* IN TOO?
I DON'T SEE WHY NOT! DIDN'T JESUS SAY TO LOVE YOUR ENEMIES?*
*CF MATT 5:44

YEAH, AND HE ALSO SAID...

"DEPART FROM ME, YOU CURSED, INTO THE ETERNAL FIRE PREPARED FOR THE DEVIL AND HIS ANGELS!"*
*MATT 25:41

SOUNDS LIKE THE DEVIL'S OUT OF LUCK!

ANYWAY, I THINK THAT IF THE DEVIL EVER ENTERED HEAVEN, HE WOULD FIND HIMSELF IN HELL.
WHY'S THAT??

BECAUSE HEAVEN IS NOTHING MORE, NOR LESS, THAN THE CLOSEST POSSIBLE UNION WITH GOD FOR ALL ETERNITY!

For someone who hates God, it would be worse than being stuck on a desert island with your worst enemy.

That's the fulfillment of my deepest desire?? Union with God?? How boring!

What did you think it would be??

Hmm, heaven...

Heaven...

Would have...

LARGE FLUFFY CATS!!!

Hmph! That's ridiculous!

Everyone knows you can't have heaven without Rocky Road ice cream!
Mmm...

Poof
Heaven is much better than that!

In fact, we couldn't be satisfied with anything less than God himself!*
*See Vol. 1 Chap. 7

As St. Augustine put it, Our hearts are restless till they rest in God.
That is, in a personal loving union with God forever!
Even in this life, our greatest pleasures come from intimate relationships with others...

Wait! Aren't we already united with God? Isn't he everywhere??

If so, then we're already in heaven, right?

SURE, GOD'S EVERYWHERE, BUT HEAVEN'S NOT!
OTHERWISE *THIS* WOULD BE HEAVEN!

UGH! GOOD POINT.
GOD IS EVERYWHERE, KEEPING EVERYTHING IN EXISTENCE BY HIS POWER...

AND ALTHOUGH WE CAN EVEN ENJOY FRIENDSHIP WITH HIM NOW BY HIS GRACE, A FRIENDSHIP THAT CONTINUES FOREVER...

HEAVEN'S MORE THAN THAT! IT'S THE ETERNAL LIFE THAT JESUS PROMISED HIS DISCIPLES; THE FACE TO FACE VISION OF GOD, WHERE THERE'S NO SADNESS OR SUFFERING!

INDEED, EYE HAS NOT SEEN NOR EAR HEARD WHAT GOD HAS PREPARED FOR THOSE WHO LOVE HIM!*
*CF. 1 COR 2:9

THIS IS ALL TOO COMPLICATED! I JUST WANT MY FAIR SHARE OF ETERNAL HAPPINESS, NOT THIS RELIGIOUS STUFF!

NONE OF US HAS A *FAIR SHARE* OF HEAVEN, SINCE NONE BUT GOD HAS A RIGHT TO LIVE A DIVINE LIFE.
SOUNDS LIKE YOU'RE OUT OF LUCK!

SO WE'RE BACK TO GOD TEASING US WITH SOMETHING WE CAN'T HAVE!

THAT'S NOT IT EITHER. WE CAN'T GET TO HEAVEN *NATURALLY*, BUT WE CAN GET THERE THROUGH *GRACE!*
...SINCE IT'S ONLY BY GRACE THAT ONE BECOMES A CHILD OF GOD, SHARING IN HIS DIVINE LIFE FOR ALL ETERNITY!
B

OTHERWISE, OUR NATURE HAS AS MUCH HOPE OF SHARING IN GOD'S LIFE AS A PLANT HAS OF SHARING IN A FAMILY DINNER...

BUT GOD'S GRACE CAN DO THE IMPOSSIBLE!

AND WHERE DOES THIS "GRACE" COME FROM?

FROM CHRIST'S SACRIFICE ON THE CROSS OF COURSE!
BY IT, HE WON MORE THAN ENOUGH GRACE FOR US ALL TO GET TO HEAVEN!

SO EVERYONE DOES GO TO HEAVEN!

IF EVERYONE WENT STRAIGHT TO HEAVEN, THEN I DON'T SEE WHY CHRIST WOULD HAVE BOTHERED TO WARN ANYONE ABOUT GOING TO HELL!

I THINK IT WAS ST. AUGUSTINE WHO SAID...

"GOD WHO CREATED YOU WITHOUT YOU WILL NOT SAVE YOU WITHOUT YOU."

SO LET'S SAY EVERYONE WHO'S MORE OR LESS GOOD GOES TO HEAVEN.
HEAVEN ISN'T FULL OF PEOPLE WHO ARE MORE OR LESS GOOD...

HEAVEN IS FOR SAINTS! AND GOD TELLS US THAT SAINTS ARE THOSE WHO LOVE HIM AND DO HIS WILL.

WELL AND GOOD IF THAT'S WHAT YOU WANT TO BELIEVE...
BUT MY GOD IS MORE INCLUSIVE THAN YOURS!

LADY, THERE'S JUST ONE GOD IN THIS UNIVERSE!

UH, DID YOU WANT YOUR BAG OF SNACK MIX NOW OR AFTER WE LAND?

THANK GOD WE'RE HERE.

Soon...
Another satisfied customer!

Remind me again why we have to lug people along with the mail?
Because the company said so?
Hey Brendan and Erc!
MC119

Pant Pant
The boss is looking for you two! He wants to see you in his office ASAP!
Thanks, Joe, we'll be right there.

Captains Brendan and Erc are here to see you sir.

Send them in, Nicki.

Captains, thank you for coming...

Tell me, what do you see when you look out into space?

A bunch of little white dots?

I'll tell you what I see... I see opportunity!

Big things are happening on Mars! The planet is on the verge of a major breakthrough, and we need a stronger presence there!

Besides, I'm hearing a lot of complaints about you, and this is your chance to redeem yourselves...

You're both to report to Mars by the end of the week!
WHAT!?!

A FEW DAYS LATER...
CHAPTER 2
GATEWAY TO PARADISE

HERE WE ARE!

OOF! UMPH!

WARNING! WARNING!
CLICK

THHPTT
?!?

010011

O MY POOR PURSIE!
SORRY, BUT THAT BAG WILL HAVE TO BE CHECKED IN!

LATER...

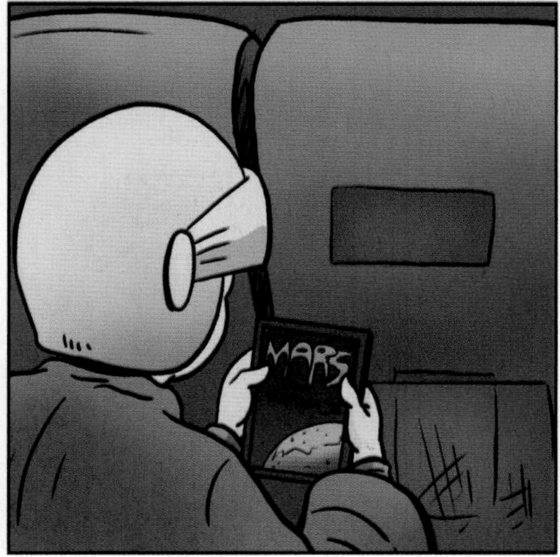
MARS

MARS
A New Paradise

FROM THE DAWN OF THE SPACE AGE, HUMANS HAVE THOUGHT OF TURNING MARS INTO ANOTHER EARTH...

BUT LACK OF RESOURCES AND TECHNOLOGY HAVE HELD BACK THAT DREAM FOR ANOTHER DAY...

AT LAST, THAT DAY HAS COME!

THREE THINGS ARE NEEDED TO BRING MARS BACK TO LIFE: HEAT, AIR, AND WATER.
RECENTLY, ROBOCO HAS PAVED THE WAY FOR ALL OF THEM...

FIRST, THE PLANET'S SURFACE WAS WARMED USING A MASSIVE SPACE MIRROR...
THEN AN ARTIFICIAL MAGNETOSPHERE WAS ESTABLISHED ON THE MARTIAN MOON PHOBUS TO KEEP THE ATMOSPHERE FROM ESCAPING INTO SPACE.

FINALLY, DRONES WERE LAUNCHED INTO VOLCANOES SCATTERED THROUGHOUT THE PLANET, CAUSING PLANET-WIDE ERUPTIONS.

THIS WILL THICKEN THE ATMOSPHERE WITHIN WEEKS, WHICH PROCESSING DRONES CAN THEN CHANGE INTO BREATHABLE AIR...

IN JUST OVER A YEAR, MARS MAY BE UNRECOGNIZABLE. NO LONGER A RED, LIFELESS PLANET, BUT A LIVING WORLD FULL OF COLOR!

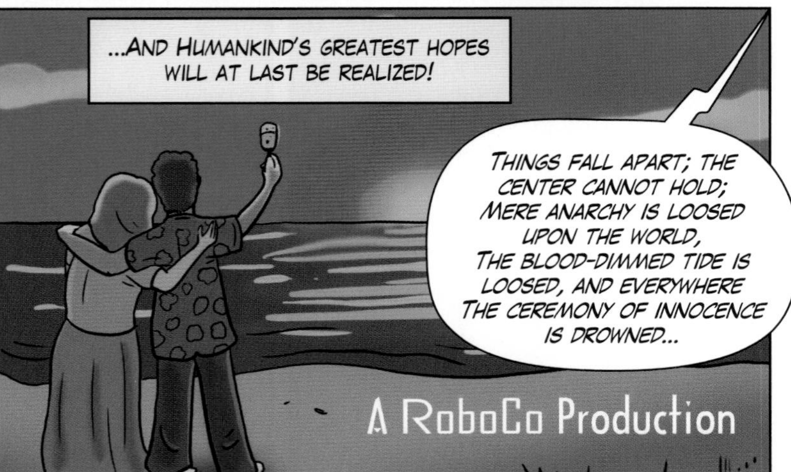
...AND HUMANKIND'S GREATEST HOPES WILL AT LAST BE REALIZED!
THINGS FALL APART; THE CENTER CANNOT HOLD; MERE ANARCHY IS LOOSED UPON THE WORLD, THE BLOOD-DIMMED TIDE IS LOOSED, AND EVERYWHERE THE CEREMONY OF INNOCENCE IS DROWNED...
A RoboCo Production

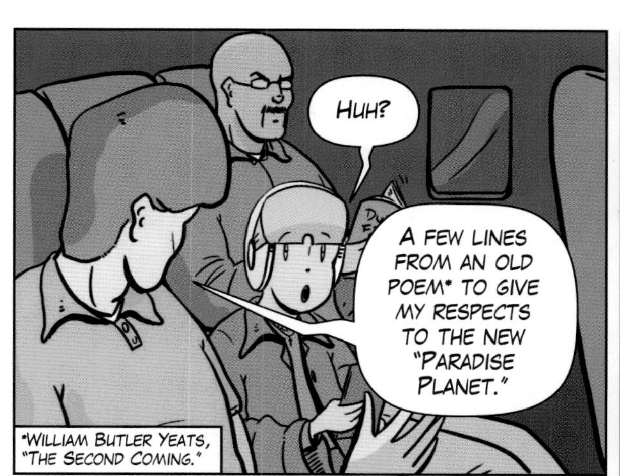

HUH?
A FEW LINES FROM AN OLD POEM* TO GIVE MY RESPECTS TO THE NEW "PARADISE PLANET."
*WILLIAM BUTLER YEATS, "THE SECOND COMING."

IT'S NO PLACE FOR CHRISTIANS, YOU KNOW.

WHAT DO YOU MEAN?

YOUR CROSS...
AREN'T YOU CHRISTIANS??

NO, WE'RE CATHOLICS!

HEH, HEH... WE'RE BOTH.

I HOPE YOU DON'T PLAN TO EVANGELIZE MARS. THERE'S NEVER BEEN A MORE GODLESS PLANET!
OH NO! OUR COMPANY IS TRANSFERRING US THERE. HOW ABOUT YOURSELF?

MY JOB IS SENDING ME TO MARS TOO.

SO WHAT DO YOU DO...
THE TROUBLE WITH YOU CATHOLICS IS THAT YOU WORK TOO HARD TO BE SAVED!

WHAT'S THAT SUPPOSED TO MEAN??

ROMANS 10:9 CLEARLY SAYS THAT *FAITH* IS ALL YOU NEED TO GET TO HEAVEN!
"IF YOU CONFESS WITH YOUR LIPS THAT JESUS IS LORD AND BELIEVE IN YOUR HEART THAT GOD RAISED HIM FROM THE DEAD, *YOU WILL BE SAVED.*"

BUT *YOU* SAY THAT A MAN HAS TO BE BAPTIZED AND JUMP THROUGH COUNTLESS HOOPS TO EVEN *HOPE* FOR SALVATION!

WE'RE ONLY REPEATING WHAT JESUS SAID...

"HE WHO BELIEVES AND IS BAPTIZED WILL BE SAVED; BUT HE WHO DOES NOT BELIEVE WILL BE CONDEMNED."*
*MARK 16:16

THEN WHY DOES PAUL SAY OTHERWISE?

I THINK HE'S EMPHASIZING THE IMPORTANCE OF FAITH IN THE LIFE OF A CHRISTIAN, SINCE, WITHOUT IT, BAPTISM WOULDN'T AMOUNT TO MUCH.

SO THOSE WHO HAVE FAITH BUT AREN'T BAPTIZED CAN BE SAVED AFTER ALL!
UM...

NO

OH? EXAMPLE ONE: THE GOOD THIEF ON THE CROSS NEXT TO JESUS. NEVER BAPTIZED, YET HE'S SAVED...

EXAMPLE TWO: THE PROPHETS, LIKE ELIJAH, WERE NEVER BAPTIZED, YET THEY WERE SAVED!

UH, THERE'S A REALLY GOOD REASON FOR THAT...

TELL 'EM BRENDAN!

WELL, IT MAY SEEM LIKE A CONTRADICTION, BUT IT'S NOT...

THE ANSWER LIES IN THERE BEING MORE THAN ONE BAPTISM.
HEY! I THOUGHT YOU COULD ONLY BE BAPTIZED ONCE!

I MEAN THAT, ASIDE FROM A BAPTISM BY WATER, THERE'S ALSO A BAPTISM OF BLOOD AND A BAPTISM OF DESIRE.

YOU BAPTIZE PEOPLE IN BLOOD?! HOW PRIMITIVE!

No, no, baptism of blood is when someone dies for Christ, even though he was never baptized with water...*
*See CCC #1258

In this way, a person is joined to the Body of Christ by faith, and the ultimate witness of that faith by martyrdom.

Then there are those who sincerely love God and repent of their sins, and so implicitly desire baptism...
These are joined to Christ by a baptism of desire.*
I wish I could be joined to a cheeseburger by just desiring it!
*See Acts 10:44 & CCC #1260

The holy prophets and the good thief would have been saved by this kind of baptism, since they had a sincere love of God and hatred for their sins.

If faith is so necessary in these baptisms, how can you baptize babies?? A child can't have faith without reason!

Nobody ever made a fuss about *circumcising* babies!

What??

I think he means that, just as circumcision made a boy part of God's chosen people, in the Old Covenant...

So in the New Covenant, children are brought into the People of God through Baptism.*
*Cf. Col 2:11

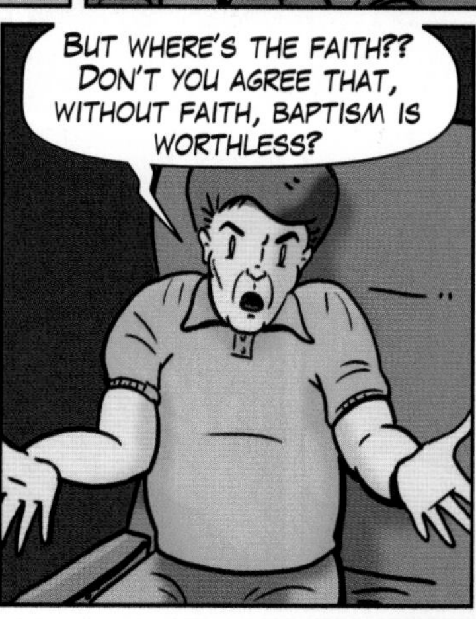

But where's the faith?? Don't you agree that, without faith, baptism is worthless?

It's in the parents, the godparents, the Church...

Just as Jesus accepted the faith of the four friends of the paralytic and forgave his sins*...
*Luke 5:20

So the faith of the Church makes up for what is lacking in the child being baptized!
Besides, the child's faith is nourished through instruction as he grows.

Ho! Ho! A slam dunk!

I'VE HAD ABOUT ENOUGH OF YOU!

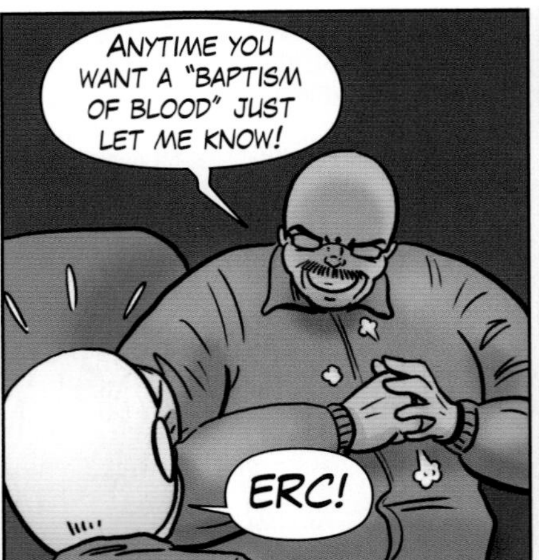
ANYTIME YOU WANT A "BAPTISM OF BLOOD" JUST LET ME KNOW!
ERC!

LET'S GO!

EXCUSE ME...

WOULD YOU LIKE ANYTHING TO DRINK?

YES, SOME GRAPE JUICE, PLEASE.

I'LL HAVE AN APPLE JUICE.
GINGER ALE FOR ME!

HERE YOU GO!
GRAPE

GINGER ALE

NO DRINKS TILL YOU BOTH SHAKE HANDS AND FORGIVE.

SORRY.
S'ALRIGHT.

I THOUGHT ONLY *SICK* PEOPLE DRANK GINGER ALE!

NEVER HEARD OF A *GROWN MAN* DRINKING GRAPE JUICE BEFORE!

LATER...
SOUNDS LIKE YOU'VE GOT IT ALL FIGURED OUT...
CHAPTER 3
DIVINE SIGNS

BUT I'M STILL NOT CONVINCED.

ROMANS 5:1 SAYS, "THEREFORE, SINCE WE ARE JUSTIFIED BY FAITH, WE HAVE PEACE WITH GOD THROUGH OUR LORD JESUS CHRIST."
HERE WE GO AGAIN!

SEE! IT'S BY FAITH THAT A MAN IS JUSTIFIED AND MADE RIGHTEOUS BEFORE GOD!
SO BAPTISM IS SUPERFLUOUS, A MERE OUTWARD PROFESSION OF THE GRACE ALREADY RECEIVED.
BUT WHERE DOES THAT GRACE COME FROM?

FROM CHRIST'S SACRIFICE ON THE CROSS, OF COURSE!
"FOR GOD SO LOVED THE WORLD THAT HE GAVE HIS ONLY SON, THAT WHOEVER BELIEVES IN HIM SHOULD NOT PERISH BUT HAVE ETERNAL LIFE.*"
*JOHN 3:16

THAT'S TRUE, BUT HOW IS THAT GRACE APPLIED TO THE INDIVIDUAL SOUL?

SIMPLE! WHENEVER SOMEONE HAS FAITH IN CHRIST, HE RECEIVES THE GRACE THAT JUSTIFIES HIM!

THAT MAY BE, BUT IT'S NOT WHAT THE FIRST CHRISTIANS BELIEVED.

FOR THEM, THE GRACES WON BY CHRIST ON THE CROSS ARE LIKE A GREAT LAKE WHOSE WATERS REACH A SOUL THROUGH THE SEVEN STREAMS OF THE SACRAMENTS.

WHAT'S A "SACRAMENT?"

IT'S A SENSIBLE SIGN, INSTITUTED BY CHRIST TO GIVE GRACE.

AS OPPOSED TO A... RIDICULOUS SIGN??

*See Vol. 1, Chap. 1

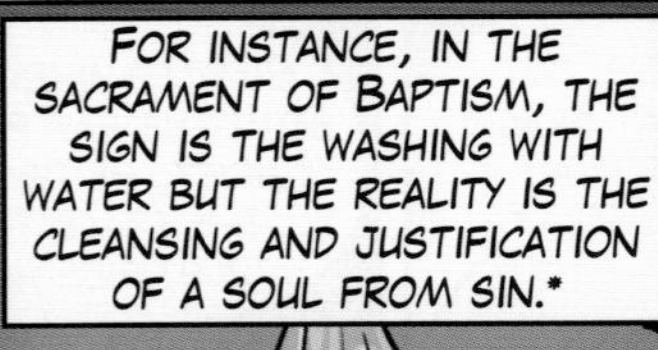

*Cf. 1 Pet 3:21

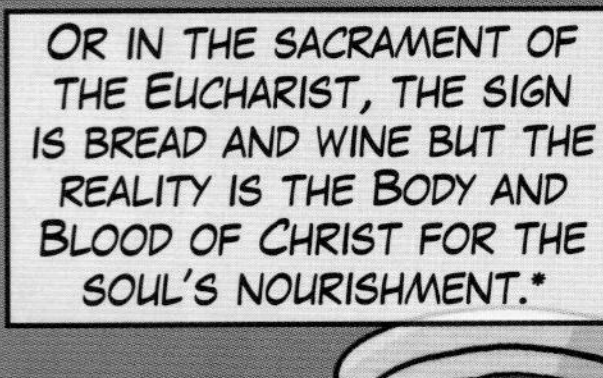

*Cf. Luke 22:19-20

*1 Pet 3:21

*John 6:51

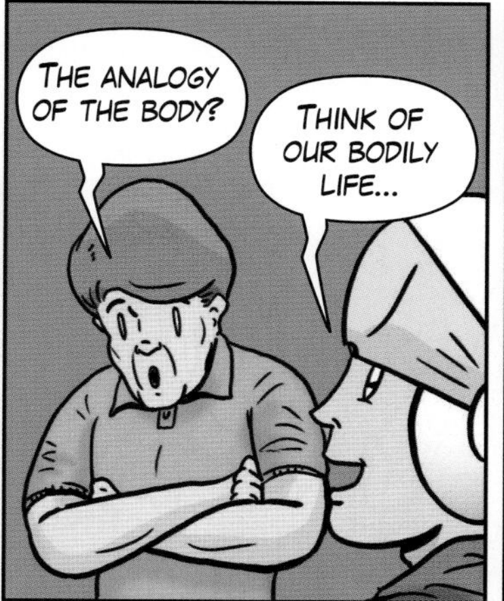

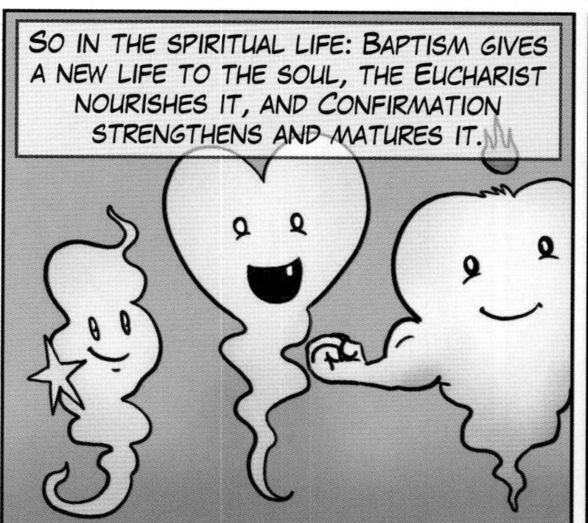

BESIDES, THERE ARE PLENTY OF CHRISTIAN WORDS THAT DON'T APPEAR IN THE BIBLE!
...LIKE "TRINITY" OR "CONSUBSTANTIAL" OR "BINGO!"

Think of it this way, Jesus Christ wants people to continue to encounter him in every age as they did back in the First Century...

So he continues to forgive sins through the sacrament of Confession, heals the sick through Anointing, lives with us and in us through the Eucharist...

Ladies and Gentlemen, we're coming in for our final approach to the Martian Orbital Platform...

OOOOH!!

What's going on down there??

Minutes later...

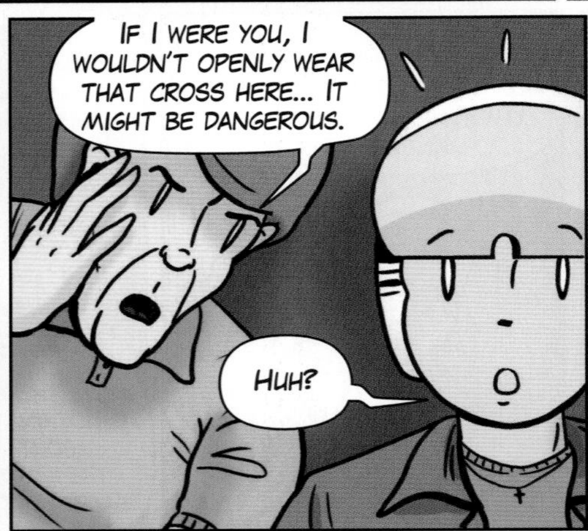
If I were you, I wouldn't openly wear that cross here... It might be dangerous.
Huh?

Why's that?

??

I hope they remembered to send someone to pick us up.

SOON...
YOU MEAN YOU DON'T FLY ANY CARGO??
CHAPTER 4
CITY OF THE GODS

NOT OUT HERE! THE FURTHEST WE FLY IS THE MOP*, SO WE'VE SPLIT THE WORK BETWEEN SHUTTLING MAIL AND CABBING PEOPLE AROUND... IT'S MORE EFFICIENT.
*MARTIAN ORBITAL PLATFORM

THERE'S OLYMPIA, "CITY OF THE GODS," THE GREATEST CITY KNOWN TO MAN!
ROBOCO.

... BIGGEST CITY EVER! BUILT ON THE HIGHEST MOUNTAIN IN THE SOLAR SYSTEM, OLYMPUS MONS!

I DIDN'T THINK THERE WAS MUCH TO ATTRACT PEOPLE TO MARS.
OH, THEY COME TO MARS FOR THE HOPE IT OFFERS! MORE THAN ANYWHERE ELSE IN THE SOLAR SYSTEM...

YEAH, YEAH, IT'S THE BIGGEST AND THE BEST!

GIMME A BREAK!

HAVE YOU HEARD OF THE PARADISE PROJECT?
THE PLAN TO TURN MARS INTO ANOTHER EARTH?

IS THAT WHAT ALL THE DUST IS ABOUT??
YEP! WHEN IT SETTLES, MARS WILL HAVE A THICKER AND WARMER ATMOSPHERE, MAKING IT EARTH-LIKE!

IMAGINE! A FRESH START ON A NEW PLANET WITHOUT ANY OF EARTH'S ENVIRONMENTAL AND SOCIAL PROBLEMS!

SURE, A REGULAR "PARADISE PLANET" MADE TO ORDER!
I'LL BELIEVE IT WHEN I SEE IT!

THE NEXT DAY...

DID YOU KNOW THAT OLYMPUS MONS IS ALSO THE LARGEST VOLCANO IN OUR SOLAR SYSTEM?
AND IT'S PROBABLY THE BIGGEST AND BEST VOLCANO THAT EVER WAS!

HELLO! ARE YOU WAITING FOR A RIDE?
I THOUGHT WE STILL HAD HALF AN HOUR TILL WE TAKE CUSTOMERS!

NO, I'M LOOKING FOR CAPTAINS BRENDAN AND ERC.
THAT'S US.

I'M SPECIAL AGENT KERR FROM THE DEPARTMENT OF MARTIAN FREEDOM AND SECURITY.

WE'RE LOOKING FOR A DANGEROUS CRIMINAL.

HAVE YOU SEEN HIM?
WANTED
NO, SORRY.

HOW ABOUT THIS MISSING WOMAN?
SORRY, THIS IS OUR FIRST DAY ON MARS!

SHOULD YOU ENCOUNTER EITHER OF THEM, PLEASE CONTACT ME IMMEDIATELY.

MY CARD.

UH, THANKS.
SO... WHAT'S HE WANTED FOR?

PERVERTING THE PEOPLE WITH FALSE IDEOLOGIES.
WHAT'S THAT MEAN?!

JUST GIVE ME A CALL IF YOU SEE THEM!

WHAT A WEIRDO.

LATER...
SUDDENLY I REALIZED...

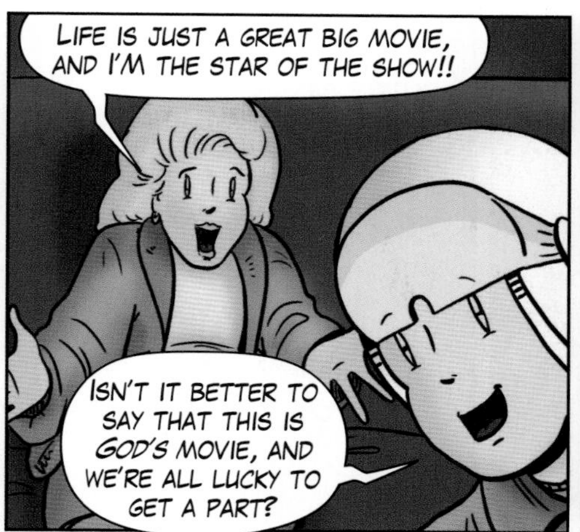
LIFE IS JUST A GREAT BIG MOVIE, AND I'M THE STAR OF THE SHOW!!
ISN'T IT BETTER TO SAY THAT THIS IS GOD'S MOVIE, AND WE'RE ALL LUCKY TO GET A PART?

GET YOUR OWN SHOW AND STAY OUTTA MINE!

...AND WHAT'S WORSE, HE GETS THE RAISE! NEVER MIND THAT I DID MOST OF THE WORK!

...OR THAT I'M SMARTER, FASTER, AND BETTER LOOKING!
THAT JERK!

"WHERE YOUR TREASURE IS, THERE WILL YOUR HEART BE ALSO."*
*MATT 6:21

ARE YOU MOCKING ME??

PROGRAMMABLE DROID DOLLS! YOU CAN'T ASK FOR A BETTER PARTNER FOR LIFE!

PROGRAMMABLE "PEOPLE"?? SOUNDS BORING!

HA! GOES TO SHOW HOW LITTLE YOU KNOW!

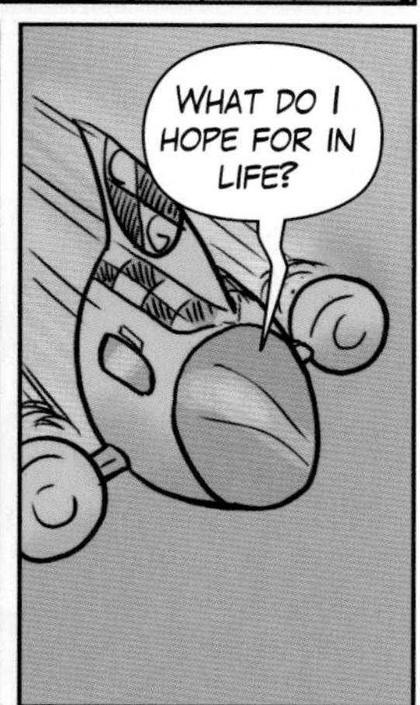
WHAT DO I HOPE FOR IN LIFE?

WHAT ELSE!? MONEY! LOTS OF MONEY!!
THIS PLANET'S A GOLDMINE, AND I'M READY TO DIG!

DO YOU REALLY THINK THAT BOZO-BOT CAN REPLACE ME!?

AT LEAST ART RESPECTS ME MORE THAN YOU EVER DID!
OH? WELL, AT LEAST MY BALINDA LISTENS TO WHATEVER I TELL HER!

SOON...
HOW'S THIS FOR RESPECT!?
I'LL TEACH YOUR BIMBO-BOT A LESSON OR TWO!

HEY, KEEP IT DOWN BACK THERE!

HOW COME I GET JUST A LITTLE BAG OF PEANUTS?? WHY CAN'T I HAVE WHAT *HE'S* HAVING??

CUZ IT'S NOT ON YOUR MENU!

"PLANET OF PEACE!" "PLANET OF HOPE!" HA!

GRUNT
PLANET OF PERVERSION IS MORE LIKE IT!

THE GOVERNMENT CONTROLS EVERYTHING! IT'S REALLY BECOME A PERFECT "RED PLANET" IF YOU GET MY MEANING.

HERE, LET ME OPEN THAT FOR YOU.
WHY?? BECAUSE YOU THINK I'M A WIMP AND CAN'T DO IT MYSELF!?

IT'S THESE #@%! GOVERNMENT PEANUT BAGS!! THEY DO IT ON PURPOSE! THEY...

BOOM

AH, HERE'S YOUR STOP.

THAT'S THE LAST NUT FOR THE DAY. LET'S GET SOMETHING TO EAT!

SHOOOP

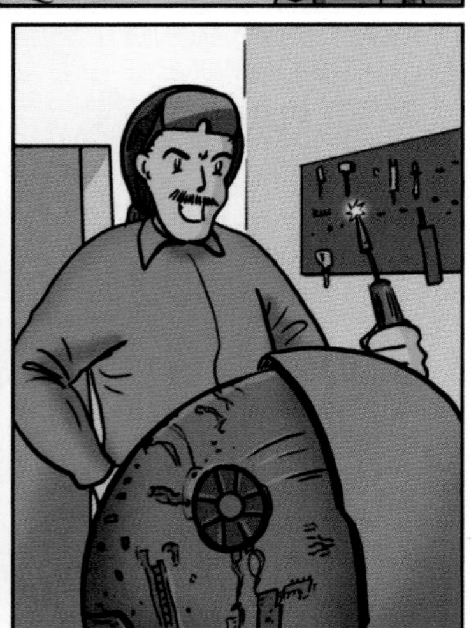

Kitty's Cat Clinic
CHAPTER 5
SOLDIERS OF CHRIST
蓝莲花
The Blue Lotus
ERC, I'VE NEVER SEEN SO MANY MISERABLE PEOPLE IN MY LIFE!
MENU
OPEN
SUPER SAKI
Blue Lotus
EXPRESS DELIVERY

蓝莲花
IF THIS IS WHAT OUR FIRST WEEK IS LIKE, WHAT DO WE HAVE TO LOOK FORWARD TO??

DON'T WORRY, YOU'LL GET USED TO IT!

THAT'S JUST WHAT I'M AFRAID OF!
DON'T YOU SEE THAT THIS ENVIRONMENT IS POISON TO OUR SOULS??

HOW LONG CAN WE HOLD OUT?? VICE BREEDS VICE!

IF ONLY FR. RAPHAEL WERE AROUND! IF ONLY I WERE STRONGER IN MY FAITH!

COME ON! DIDN'T YOU GET ALL THE STRENGTH YOU NEED AT YOUR CONFIRMATION?

WHAT DO YOU MEAN?

O YE OF LITTLE FAITH! ISN'T CONFIRMATION THE "SACRAMENT OF STRENGTH?"
HUH?

DIDN'T YOU GET THE HOLY SPIRIT AT CONFIRMATION? AND DOESN'T THAT MAKE ALL THE DIFFERENCE?

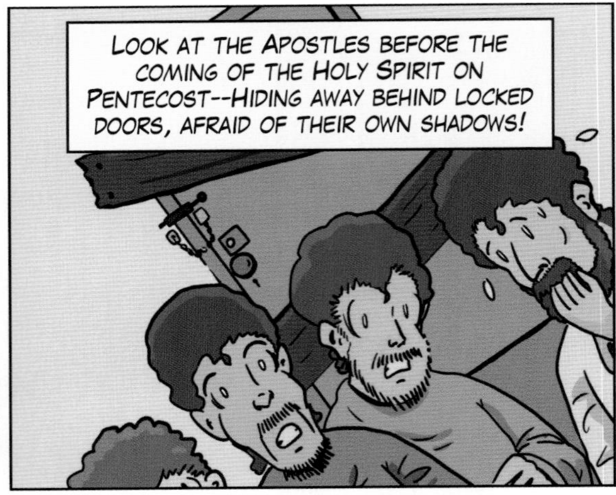
LOOK AT THE APOSTLES BEFORE THE COMING OF THE HOLY SPIRIT ON PENTECOST--HIDING AWAY BEHIND LOCKED DOORS, AFRAID OF THEIR OWN SHADOWS!

LOOK AT THEM AFTER--BOLD MISSIONARIES, CONVERTING THE WORLD TO CHRIST, HAPPILY ENDURING PRISON, TORTURE AND DEATH!

I DON'T KNOW, ERC... I DON'T FEEL VERY BOLD.

BESIDES, THE APOSTLES HAD A COMMUNITY OF CHRISTIANS, THEY HAD THE MASS, THEY WERE FULL OF THE HOLY SPIRIT...

WE'RE OUT IN THE MIDDLE OF NOWHERE, SURROUNDED BY A STRANGE PEOPLE, AND I'VE YET TO SEE A CATHOLIC CHURCH ANYWHERE.

DOESN'T MATTER!
WHAT DO YOU MEAN?! THESE ARE OUR SOULS WE'RE TALKING ABOUT!

LOOK, IF THERE'S ONE THING I REMEMBER FROM MY CONFIRMATION CLASS IT'S THAT CONFIRMATION MAKES YOU A SOLDIER OF CHRIST.

NOW, EVERY SOLDIER'S GOT A MISSION TO DO, AND WE'RE NO DIFFERENT...

SO IF WE'RE OUT HERE, MILLIONS OF MILES FROM HOME, THERE'S A REASON!

REMEMBER THE STORY OF THE HOLY SPIRIT SETTING ASIDE BARNABAS AND SAUL FOR A MISSION?*
*ACTS 13:2

DO YOU THINK THEY WERE TOLD WHAT THAT MISSION WAS? NO! THEY WENT, TRUSTING THAT THE HOLY SPIRIT WOULD GUIDE THEM!

WELL, GOD SENT US HERE, AND HE'LL TAKE CARE OF US...

IT'S THAT SIMPLE.

SLURP
MUNCH

BUT HOW DO YOU EXPLAIN MY LACK OF COURAGE? MAYBE SOMETHING WENT WRONG AND I WASN'T ACTUALLY CONFIRMED!

WHAT? YOU THINK FR. RAPHAEL BOTCHED THE RITE??

I THINK HE'S DONE A FEW CONFIRMATIONS IN HIS DAY!

MAYBE IT WAS MY FAULT? MAYBE I DIDN'T INTEND TO BE CONFIRMED, OR MAYBE I WAS IN A STATE OF SIN...?

THAT'S RIDICULOUS! IF YOU DIDN'T INTEND TO BE CONFIRMED YOU'D KNOW IT!
AND ALL YOUR SINS WERE WASHED AWAY IN BAPTISM, REMEMBER?

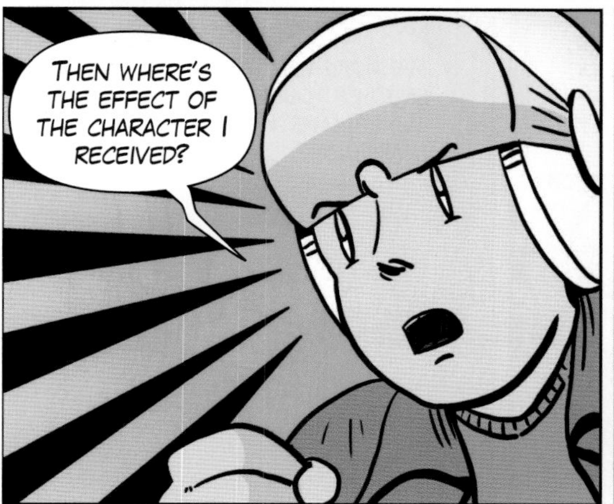
THEN WHERE'S THE EFFECT OF THE CHARACTER I RECEIVED?

WHAT CHARACTER? YOU'RE STILL THE SAME BRENDAN TO ME!
I MEAN THE INDELIBLE MARK STAMPED ON MY SOUL AT CONFIRMATION!

?

YOU KNOW! IT'S THE REASON YOU CAN'T BE BAPTIZED OR CONFIRMED TWICE!

REMIND ME.

WELL, IN BAPTISM IT'S A MARK OF BELONGING TO CHRIST, MAKING US ABLE TO RECEIVE THE OTHER SACRAMENTS.

OH! AND YOU GET IT AGAIN WHEN YOU'RE CONFIRMED?

No, when you're Confirmed, you get *another* character that strengthens the soul to profess the Faith boldly.

It also marks you as a soldier of Christ, kind of like the tattoos that Roman soldiers had to identify them.
PROPERTY
OF ROME

Well, why isn't it doing its job? What's wrong with me??

I don't know, but I doubt this thing changes your character so soon...

If you're usually a coward, only a miracle is going to make you act differently overnight!

Anyway, I'm sure that mark is there, and the strength that goes with it... it's just waiting for the right time to come out.
I hope you're right!

Speaking of strength, we'd better find a church--Tomorrow's Sunday, and I'm starving for Communion!
Shouldn't be a problem in a city this big!

After that, we can think about our mission and how to bring Christ to these people.

Simple!

We fake an emergency and, as the ship plummets, our passengers will have a conversion experience they'll never forget!

We hope you enjoyed your meal! Have a nice day!

Oh! Fortune cookies!
BILL

"Courage! Adventure is just around the corner."
That's interesting!

"Do yourself a favor... "

"Diet!"

The Next Day...
I can't believe it!!

Not a single church on the map! Catholic, Protestant or Orthodox! Nothing!

Hmph! Not so much as a Synagogue, Mosque, or Kingdom Hall for that matter!

This "city of the gods" sure is godless!

What are we going to do, Erc??
It's one thing to be a soldier of Christ, but quite another to be cut off from your supply line!

I still say, God's in charge, even in godlessness.

Hm, that would make a great fortune cookie...

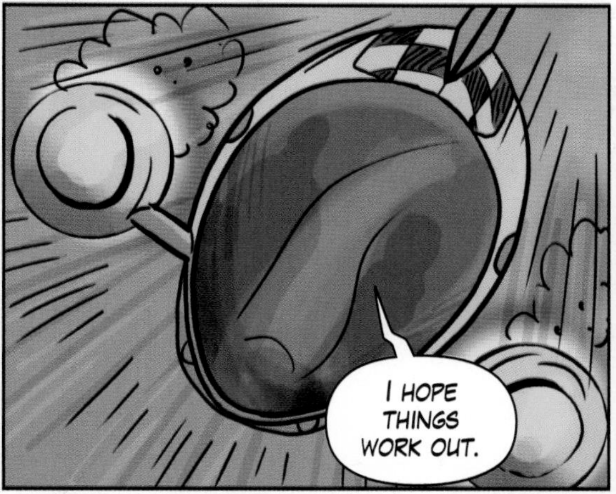

I hope things work out.

Soon...
...I've got connections everywhere! Anything and everything you could possibly ask for, I can get ya for a price!

Why, just last year, I managed to dig up an old TS38b for a company that needed it!*
*See Vol 2.

Bet you thought those ships were long extinct!

Can you find us a Mass?

A WHAT??

A CATHOLIC MASS. CAN YOU FIND US A MASS?

NEVER HEARD OF IT! HOW ABOUT A *MAST* INSTEAD? I CAN GET 'EM IN ANY SHAPE, SIZE AND COLOR!

NO THANKS.

SECTOR FOUR, 57TH AND 6TH, PLEASE.

YOU SOUND LIKE SOMEONE WHO KNOWS HIS WAY AROUND. CAN YOU HELP US?

WE'VE BEEN LOOKING EVERYWHERE FOR A CATHOLIC CHURCH AND HAVEN'T HAD ANY LUCK.

YOU MUST BE NEW HERE TO WASTE YOUR TIME LOOKING FOR A CHURCH ON MARS.
WHAT DO YOU MEAN?

I MEAN THERE ARE NO CHURCHES IN PARADISE!

CHAPTER 6
THE BREAD OF LIFE
Hey, don't cry! Think of all the benefits of not going to church anymore...
SOB!
We're doomed! How can we survive without the Mass!?

More sleep on Sundays, plenty of extra time to do what you want, no long-winded sermons.

All the benefits of the universe couldn't make up for the one thing I'd be missing!
What's there to miss!?

Jesus Christ in the Eucharist!

Is that all?? You don't need a *church* to find Christ!

Why, he's just as present here as anywhere!

It's true that as *God* he's everywhere, but he's in the Eucharist in a special way...

There he's *physically* present!

Do you really believe that?? What would put such a silly idea into your head?

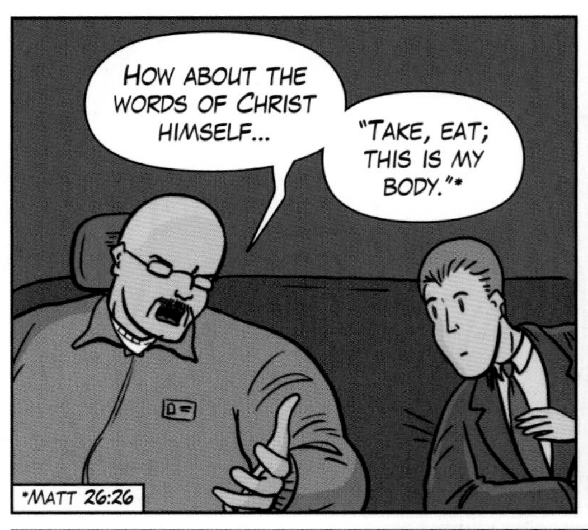
How about the words of Christ himself...
"Take, eat; this is my body."*
*Matt 26:26

He meant those words *figuratively*.

Then why does he say elsewhere, "The bread which I shall give for the life of the world is my flesh"?*
*John 6:51

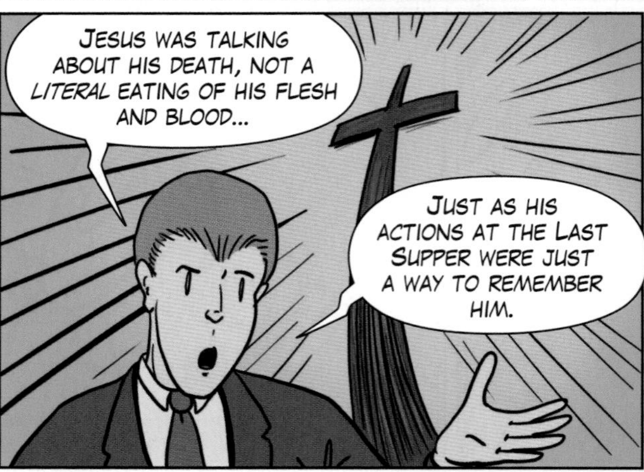
Jesus was talking about his death, not a *literal* eating of his flesh and blood...
Just as his actions at the Last Supper were just a way to remember him.

I can think of better ways to remember him!

...A statue or a painting would be much more permanent than a meal!
OOOoh

Who are you to decide what memento Christ would leave behind??
The Apostles who were there didn't seem to think it was just a memento...

Weren't these the same apostles who misunderstood Christ's words before?

ZZZZZZ
When he told them that Lazarus was dead, they thought he meant he was only sleeping.*
*John 11:12

And when he spoke to them about the "leaven of the Pharisees," they thought he was talking about mere bread.*
*Matt 16:7

Both times they misunderstood him by taking his words *literally*, just as you're doing now!

I'd like to see those passages.
Hm...

OH!

WHAT? WHAT!?
OH?
THERE'S A BIG DIFFERENCE BETWEEN THOSE PASSAGES AND THE ONE IN CHAPTER 6 OF JOHN'S GOSPEL ABOUT THE EUCHARIST...

IN THE PASSAGES WHERE JESUS' APOSTLES MISUNDERSTAND HIM, HE QUICKLY CORRECTS THEM...

SO IN THE CASE OF LAZARUS, HE TELLS THEM PLAINLY, "LAZARUS IS DEAD."*
*JOHN 11:14

AND WITH THE LEAVEN OF THE PHARISEES, HE SAYS, "HOW IS IT THAT YOU FAIL TO PERCEIVE THAT I DID NOT SPEAK ABOUT BREAD?"*
*MATT 16:11

BUT WHEN HE SAYS, "THE BREAD WHICH I SHALL GIVE FOR THE LIFE OF THE WORLD IS MY FLESH"* AND EVERYONE IS SHOCKED, ASKING, "HOW CAN THIS MAN GIVE US HIS FLESH TO EAT?"...
*JOHN 6:51

...JESUS *DOESN'T* CORRECT THEM!

IN FACT, HE SOLEMNLY REPEATS HIMSELF: "TRULY, TRULY, I SAY TO YOU, UNLESS YOU EAT THE FLESH OF THE SON OF MAN AND DRINK HIS BLOOD, YOU HAVE NO LIFE IN YOU".*
*JOHN 6:53

THAT'S NOT ALL!
THE WORD CHANGES IN THE GREEK FROM "*PHAGO*," WHICH IS A GENERIC WORD FOR "EAT" IN "UNLESS YOU EAT THE FLESH OF THE SON OF MAN..."*
*JOHN 6:53

TO "*TROGO*," MEANING "TO GNAW OR CHEW" IN "HE WHO EATS MY FLESH AND DRINKS MY BLOOD HAS ETERNAL LIFE"*
*JOHN 6:54

EMPHASIZING THE REALITY OF THE EATING!

WELL SAID.
YOU KNOW GREEK, ERC??

IT'S IN THE FOOTNOTES.

But if that's the case, then Jesus is sanctioning cannibalism!

No, since he gives us his flesh and blood to eat in the form of *bread and wine.*

So you're saying that bread and wine become the *real* flesh and blood of Jesus Christ??

Yes, it's a mystery how such a thing can take place...
But it's not beyond God's power!

So God makes something be both true and false at the same time and the same way?

Um...
I think not! Either it's bread and wine or it's Christ's body and blood... it can't be both!

You're right...
What!?

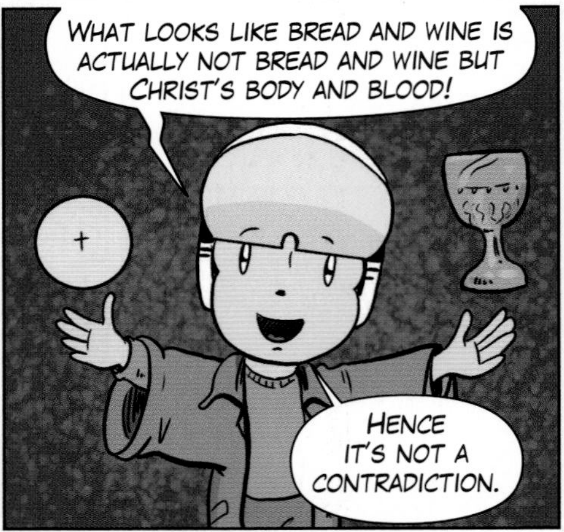
What looks like bread and wine is actually not bread and wine but Christ's body and blood!
Hence it's not a contradiction.

Explain.

We believe that the whole substance of bread changes into the substance of Christ's body and the whole substance of wine into his blood...

What's a substance again?

It's what a thing is.
Gee! That helps!

So, if you ask "What is that?" the answer is "A man."

No matter what color he is, or outfit he's wearing, or style of hair he has, it doesn't change the fact that he is *substantially* a man.

His color, outfit, and hair style are accidental to his being a man, since they don't affect his "man-ness."
Nor is a fat man more of a man than a skinny man, since "fat" and "skinny" are also accidental to what a man is.

In the case of the Eucharist, the only thing changing is the substance of the bread and wine...
Their *accidents*--shape, color, taste, smell-- all stay the same!

Hence we call this change *transubstantiation*...
Because the whole substance of the bread and wine changes into the body and blood of Christ.

But if you can't sense the change, then how do you know it really takes place?

Because we believe him who said, "This is my body" and "This is my blood."

If God's own Word can't be trusted, then who can?

Okay, I'm convinced...
What? That Christ is really present in the Eucharist?

No, that you're Catholics. Please land at the nearest pad.

Do you mind stepping outside?

Why? What's this all about!?
I'll explain in a minute.

Stand right here, please.

What are you doing!?
Scanning for bugs.

Something in your pocket. What do you have there?
BEEEEEEP

One of Kerr's cards...

I thought so. A tracking device.
RIP

You won't be needing this anymore.
If you don't want a punch in the nose, you'd better tell us what you're up to and fast!

You're looking for a Mass and I know where you can find one.

But you said there aren't any churches on Mars!
There aren't any that you can find, but there are a few underground, in hiding...

I trust you can keep a secret.
Sure.
Yes.

What I'm about to tell you is extremely sensitive information...

Go to the Pierced Pelican this evening and order the Deluxe Lamb Supper. Tell them Alex sent you.

Lamb!? Yuck!

THAT EVENING...
CHAPTER 7
AT THE PIERCED PELICAN
The Pierced Pelican

THIS IS MORE LIKE IT! FINALLY SOMEWHERE THAT FEELS LIKE HOME!

BUT WHY ALL THE SECRECY? IF THERE'S AN UNDERGROUND CHURCH, WHY NOT JUST GIVE US A TIME AND ADDRESS FOR THE MASS?
NEW!

HI! READY TO ORDER?

YES, WE'D LIKE THE DELUXE LAMB SUPPER.

SORRY, THAT'S NOT ON THE MENU.
THANK YOU, GOD!

BUT... BUT ALEX SENT US!
OH! YOU KNOW ALEX?

I'LL BE RIGHT BACK.
WAIT, I'D LIKE TO ORDER A BEER!

THE SUPPER ALREADY COMES WITH A DRINK...

A REFRESHING MINT TEA!

MINUTES LATER...
HERE YOU GO...

TWO SUPPERS WITH SPECIAL TEA.

LET ME KNOW IF YOU NEED ANYTHING ELSE.

ERC, LOOK AT THE TEA!
I DON'T WANT TO LOOK AT TEA, I WANT TO LOOK AT BE--

OH!

9pm Sector 3, 1238 Wells Drive "Christ is King!"

WHAT DO YOU THINK?
IF THEIR TEA CAN TALK, WHAT MUST THEIR BEER DO!?

LATER...
DING DONG

WHAT'S THE GOOD WORD?
1238
UH...

CHRIST IS KING?
1238

WELCOME!
YOU!

GO DOWN THOSE STAIRS. FATHER IS ABOUT TO START.

DING
DING

GASP!

ERC, THAT'S THE WANTED MAN!

LOOKS LIKE A PRIEST TO ME!

THANK YOU, LORD!

EXCUSE ME. FR. MIKE WANTS TO MEET YOU BOTH.

BRENDAN AND ERC, THANKS FOR COMING! PLEASE HAVE A SEAT.
HOW DO YOU KNOW OUR NAMES?

DEACON ALEX UPDATES ME ON ALL OUR GUESTS. BESIDES, THERE AREN'T THAT MANY OF US IN THE UNDERGROUND CHURCH!

ALEX IS A DEACON??
AND YOU? AREN'T YOU A WANTED CRIMINAL?

HA HA HA HA! YES, AND YOU'VE JUST ASSISTED ME IN ONE OF MY WORST CRIMES!

WHAT DO YOU MEAN??

I MEAN YOU'VE COME TO A PLANET WHERE PUBLIC WORSHIP IS OUTLAWED, RELIGIOUS LEADERS ARE BANNED, AND EVEN PERSONAL FAITH IS HELD SUSPECT...
ALL IN HOPES OF MAKING A PERFECT PARADISE.

HERE'S A SMALL SAMPLE OF THE PROPAGANDA THAT'S REGULARLY FED TO THE PEOPLE.

Are Christians Human?

A TALE OF TWO TREES!
Christians come from **another** evolutionary tree, inferior to modern humans!
Homo Stultis
Homo Sapiens

NEEDS MORE STORY!
FLIP FLIP FLIP

WE'RE DETERMINED TO FIGHT BACK! WE'VE PUT TOGETHER A VIDEO RESPONSE, HOPING TO TRANSMIT IT ILLEGALLY. ONLY THING WE NEED TO BROADCAST IS *ALTITUDE*...
SO WE STARTED A NOVENA, AND GOD SENT US TWO PILOTS AND A SHIP!

HOW CAN WE HELP?

THE BROADCAST IS SCHEDULED FOR PENTECOST. IN THE MEANTIME, I COULD USE SOME HELP MINISTERING TO MY FLOCK, IF YOU DON'T MIND FLYING ME AROUND?
NO PROBLEM!

WHAT'S A NOVENA?

ARE YOU SURE YOU'RE CATHOLIC?

Chapter 8
A Perfect Paradise

SHHH, LET'S GO!
WHERE ARE WE GOING?

WATERSON AVENUE IN SECTOR 4... I'M HEARING CONFESSIONS THERE TODAY.

CNC43, WE'VE GOT AN EMERGENCY PICKUP IN YOUR AREA.
BLIP
WHAT'S THE PROBLEM?

THE GOVERNOR'S SHUTTLE IS DOWN AND HE NEEDS A LIFT. PLEASE RE-ROUTE IMMEDIATELY!
WE'RE ON IT!

WHAT ARE WE GOING TO DO ABOUT FATHER?
BLIP

DON'T WORRY ABOUT ME. I'M SAFER IN HERE THAN OUT THERE!
ARE YOU NUTS?? ISN'T THE GOVERNOR AFTER YOU?

YES, BUT HE'LL NEVER THINK OF LOOKING FOR ME UNDER HIS VERY NOSE!
CLICK

OOF! I'M GETTING TOO OLD FOR THIS.

LET'S GO! WE'VE GOT AN IMPORTANT MEETING ON THE MOP.
DON'T I KNOW YOU?
YES, SIR.

WE MET A COUPLE OF WEEKS AGO, ON OUR FIRST DAY ON MARS.

OH! YOU'RE NEW TO OUR PLANET?
YES.
YOU COULDN'T HAVE COME AT A BETTER TIME! STOP THE SHUTTLE! STOP, HOVER, AND DRINK IN THE *SPLENDOR* WE'VE CREATED!

SEE HOW WELL ORDERED OUR CITY IS! THERE ARE WHOLE COUNTRIES ON EARTH THAT CAN'T COMPARE IN SIZE AND MAGNIFICENCE!

SEE THAT LAKE? IT'S A TECHNOLOGICAL MASTERPIECE!
WHAT'S SO GREAT ABOUT IT?

TRILLIONS OF TONS OF ICE WERE FLOWN IN AND MELTED TO CREATE IT! WITHOUT THAT WATER, *NOTHING* COULD SURVIVE IN THIS DESERT.

AND THE AIR SHIELD ENCLOSING OLYMPIA? LARGEST AIR SHIELD IN THE UNIVERSE! A GREAT FEAT OF ENGINEERING AND TECHNOLOGY!

BUT BEST OF ALL, LOOK AT THE CLOUDS SURROUNDING OLYMPIA, WHICH ARE ALREADY DISSIPATING...

I'M SURE YOU'RE AWARE OF THE PARADISE PROJECT--MAKING MARS AN EARTH-LIKE PARADISE.
YES, WE'VE HEARD OF IT.

IT'S A TOTAL SUCCESS!
WHAT?!

Thanks to our Space Mirror constantly heating the planet, Mars hit an equatorial temperature of 75°F twelve hours ago, with an air density like that of Earth!

There are even signs of rivers starting to form!
That's amazing!

It's just the start of what we're able to do! Soon Mars will be a lush Paradise with everything that anyone could ever ask for right at his or her fingertips!

Everything but a church!

ERC!!

HA HA HA
HA HA HA HA

Let's go! We've got a meeting to catch.

Sure, some fools think that a world without churches is missing something...

But look at Earth's history and the damage religion has done there!
Here we have a chance to make a *perfect* society full of peace and happiness--the very thing that religions pretend to offer!

Why, we've already eliminated poverty, hunger, and most diseases!
That may be, but I haven't seen much peace or happiness among most of the people we've met.

Do you think they'd be better off with churches, guilt trips, and wars??

I think they'd be better off if their souls were as cared for as their bodies.

WHAT'S THAT MEAN?

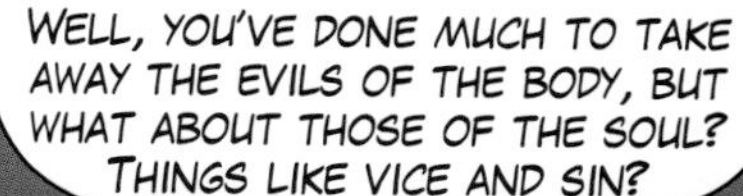
WELL, YOU'VE DONE MUCH TO TAKE AWAY THE EVILS OF THE BODY, BUT WHAT ABOUT THOSE OF THE SOUL? THINGS LIKE VICE AND SIN?

VICE? SIN?? THESE ARE ARCHAIC CONCEPTS FROM EARTH'S DARK AGES. WE'RE BEYOND ALL THAT!

IS GOD ALSO BEYOND ALL THAT??

UH, WHAT IS SIN?

IT'S AN OFFENSE AGAINST GOD AND HIS LAWS THAT LEADS TO OUR MISERY.

IF YOU THINK OF GOD'S LAWS AS HIS INSTRUCTION MANUAL FOR HAPPINESS, THEN TO SIN IS TO ACT AGAINST THESE DIRECTIONS AND END UP MISERABLE!*
*SEE VOL. 1 CHAP. 7

YEAH, SIN IS THE WORST THING IN THE UNIVERSE!

REALLY? WORSE THAN A BAD HAIR DAY??

WORSE THAN LETTING A CRIMINAL GET AWAY?

WORSE THAN LOSING AN ONLY CHILD?

UH...

...WORSE THAN WASHING YOUR GUN IN THE LAUNDRY?

IT'S WORSE THAN ALL THOSE BECAUSE IT WRECKS THE HARMONY OF THE UNIVERSE AND FRIENDSHIP WITH GOD!
...AND WHO WANTS GOD FOR AN ENEMY??

THAT'S RIDICULOUS! HOW CAN THE ORDER OF THE UNIVERSE POSSIBLY BE AFFECTED BY A SO-CALLED SIN?

THINK ABOUT THE HISTORY OF HUMANITY, FILLED WITH GREED, WAR, INJUSTICE AND A HOST OF OTHER EVILS...

NOW, WE BELIEVE THAT GOD CREATED MAN IN A STATE OF PEACE AND HARMONY, AND THAT ALL THESE THINGS ENTERED THE WORLD BECAUSE OF ONE ACT OF DISOBEDIENCE AGAINST GOD.*
*SEE VOL. 2, CHAP. 7

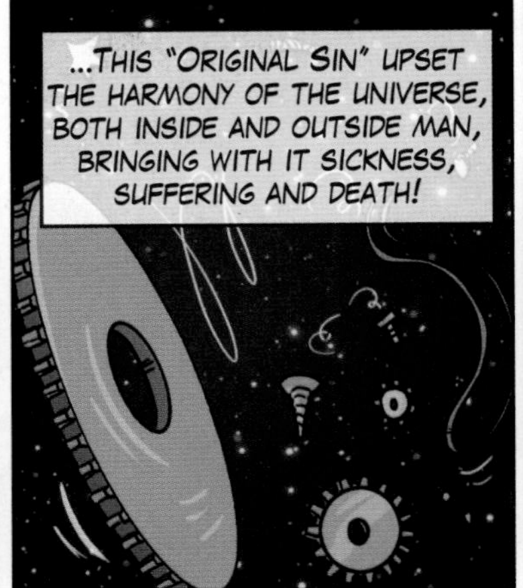
...THIS "ORIGINAL SIN" UPSET THE HARMONY OF THE UNIVERSE, BOTH INSIDE AND OUTSIDE MAN, BRINGING WITH IT SICKNESS, SUFFERING AND DEATH!

AND EVEN NOW WE'RE FREE TO CHOOSE WHETHER TO BRING CHAOS OR HARMONY INTO THIS UNIVERSE, SIMPLY BY OUR ACTIONS FOR OR AGAINST GOD'S LAWS.

IN OTHER WORDS, WE ALL PUT INGREDIENTS INTO THE "SOUP OF THE UNIVERSE"...

EITHER WE MAKE IT BETTER BY OUR GOOD ACTS, OR WE MAKE IT WORSE BY OUR BAD. EITHER WAY, WE'RE IN THIS TOGETHER!
MOTOR OIL

I DON'T BELIEVE THESE LAWS EXIST, NOR THESE "SINS" AGAINST THEM.

IF THEY DID, EVERYONE WOULD KNOW THEM, BUT EACH RELIGION SAYS SOMETHING DIFFERENT ABOUT WHAT GOD CONSIDERS A "SIN"!

BESIDES, IF THEY **DID** EXIST, THERE WOULD BE PUNISHMENTS THAT GO WITH BREAKING THEM, AS WITH ALL LAWS...

BUT PLENTY OF PEOPLE LIVE IMMORAL LIVES AND DIE RICH AND HAPPY!

SINCE YOU KNOW WHAT AN IMMORAL PERSON LOOKS LIKE, YOU MUST ALSO KNOW GOD'S LAWS!

I SPEAK OF A PURELY HYPOTHETICAL SITUATION...

LOOK, ANY CHILD KNOWS RIGHT FROM WRONG AND WHEN HE'S PLAYING FAIR OR CHEATING!
WE ALL COME WITH CONSCIENCES, AND THAT'S WHAT ACCUSES OR DEFENDS US BEFORE GOD.

ALSO, GOD HAS REVEALED HIS LAWS TO MEN, GIVING US THE "INSTRUCTION MANUAL," IF YOU WILL, AND THESE CAN BE FOUND EASILY ENOUGH FOR THOSE WHO SEARCH.*
*SEE VOL. 1, CHAP. 7

AND GOD'S PUNISHMENTS EXIST TOO!
THOSE SO-CALLED HAPPY PEOPLE WHO ARE LIVING CONTRARY TO GOD'S LAWS...

PAT PAT PAT
ARE THEY AT PEACE WITH THEMSELVES AND THEIR SURROUNDINGS? ARE THEY SATISFIED WITH THEIR LIVES?

SURE! THEY'RE HAPPY! THEY HAVE WHAT THEY WANT IN LIFE!
HAPPY PILLS
HAPPY PATCH
AS FOR PEACE AND JOY... YOU CAN GET THEM IN PILL FORM OR PATCH! WHATEVER MOOD YOU WANT CAN BE BOUGHT!

BUT THIS PEACE CAN'T BE BOUGHT! THIS JOY LASTS REGARDLESS OF CHANGING MOODS AND ENVIRONMENTS!
SUPPOSE GOD HAS LAID DOWN CERTAIN RULES AND OBLIGATIONS, AND SUPPOSE IT REALLY IS A SIN TO BREAK THEM...

WHAT DOES IT MATTER?? DOES GOD REALLY CARE IF I CHEAT SOMEONE? DOES IT MATTER IF I GO TO CHURCH OR SLEEP IN?

ONLY A SMALL-MINDED GOD WOULD BE BOTHERED BY THE WAY I CHOOSE TO LIVE MY LIFE!

NOT A "SMALL-MINDED" BUT A "BIG-HEARTED" GOD!
A GOD WHO LOVES US ENOUGH TO WANT THE BEST FOR US.

ONE WHO WAS WILLING TO DIE ON A CROSS TO SHOW US HIS LOVE AND THE GREAT EVIL OF SIN.

SEE! THIS IS THE VERY THING WE'RE ELIMINATING ON MARS, FOR THE GOOD OF THE PEOPLE!

WHAT'S THAT SUPPOSED TO MEAN?

I MEAN YOU RELIGIOUS FANATICS ARE ALL ALIKE...

Brainwashed to believe that certain acts are "sinful," and lead to misery...
While others are "virtuous," and make you happy!

Here we want a society of happy, guilt-free people who can define their own moral values!

I thought only psychopaths were "guilt-free!"
You know, guilt isn't always a bad thing...

It can be a sign of a healthy conscience--the way pain is a sign that a body is working as it should.

So you admit that you *want* people to live in pain!
The truth is that you're enslaved to your guilt and can't stand seeing people who are free!

No, that's not...
QUIET!

That's enough, thank you!

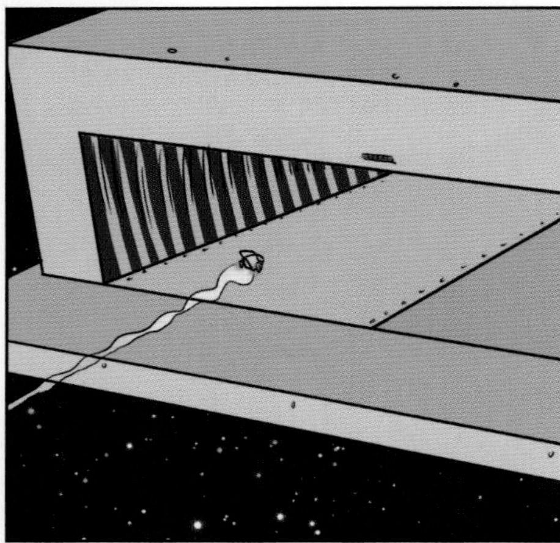

You're going to let them go??
Patience, Kerr...

Chapter 9
Confessions of a Priest
What a bunch of jerks!
Don't be too hard on them, they're already receiving their punishment.

What punishment?

If you think about it, sin is a kind of idolatry, with the sinner turning from the True God to a false one to try to satisfy his deepest desires.

Or as Scripture puts it, they "went after empty idols, and became empty themselves."*
*Jer 2:5 (NAB)

Besides cutting off friendship with God, sin darkens the mind and corrupts a person's desires, leading to more sin and misery.

Like an alcohol addiction... the more they drink, the more they're prone to keep drinking and the further they fall.

I never thought of it that way.
Sounds hopeless!

As long as there's life in the body there's always hope. A good dose of repentance and a sincere Confession can do wonders!

You think people like *that* are going to repent??
...They don't even think they've done anything wrong!

Don't underestimate God's grace!

Reminds me of a young woman I met a couple of years ago, before the anti-religion laws were enacted...

I was in the middle of hearing confessions when I met her...
CREAK

Can you really forgive sins??

What do you think I'm doing in here, handing out hot dogs??

Do you think you're God?? Only God can forgive sins!

Lady, if I thought I were God, I'd be in a padded cell, not a confessional!
Come back in a couple of hours when I'm done and I'll be happy to answer all your questions then, okay?

I didn't expect to see her again, but a few hours later she was back.

So did you want to go to confession?

I'd much rather skip the middle-man and confess directly to God!

You're not the only one! Problem is, that's not the way God set things up.

You don't think I can confess directly to God??
Sure you can! You can even find forgiveness, provided you have a perfect contrition...

What's that mean?

It means that you have to be sorry for your sins not out of fear but from a great love for God!
Oh!

THOUGH EVEN THEN, IF YOU TRULY LOVED GOD YOU'D *STILL* WANT TO CONFESS YOUR SINS TO A PRIEST.
WHY'S THAT?

BECAUSE THAT'S THE *ORDINARY* WAY GOD FORGIVES SINS!

BESIDES, IF YOU DIDN'T HEAR A PRIEST TELL YOU THAT YOUR SINS WERE FORGIVEN, HOW WOULD YOU KNOW IT FOR SURE UNLESS GOD TOLD YOU?

LOOK, IF YOU BELIEVE THAT JESUS IS GOD MADE MAN, THEN THERE'S NO DENYING THAT HE GAVE THE SACRAMENT OF CONFESSION TO FORGIVE OUR SINS.

AND HE GAVE THIS GREAT POWER NOT TO ANGELS BUT TO HIS APOSTLES IN THE UPPER ROOM WHEN HE BREATHED ON THEM AND SAID:

RECEIVE THE HOLY SPIRIT. IF YOU FORGIVE THE SINS OF ANY, THEY ARE FORGIVEN; IF YOU RETAIN THE SINS OF ANY, THEY ARE RETAINED.*

*JOHN 20:22

IF HE GAVE THIS POWER TO HIS APOSTLES, HOW DO *YOU* PRESUME TO FORGIVE SINS?? YOU'RE NOT AN APOSTLE!

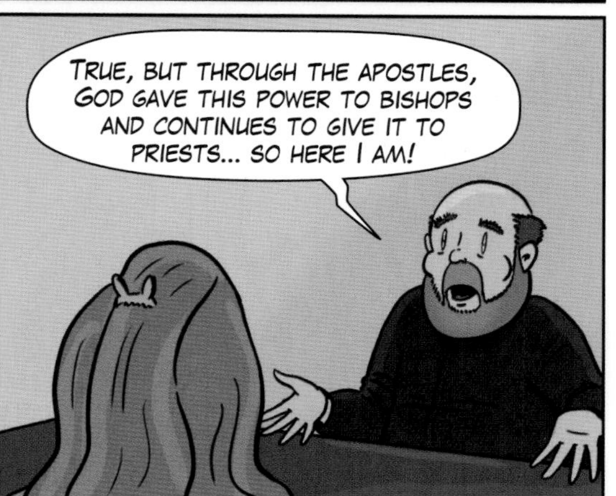
TRUE, BUT THROUGH THE APOSTLES, GOD GAVE THIS POWER TO BISHOPS AND CONTINUES TO GIVE IT TO PRIESTS... SO HERE I AM!

BESIDES, IT MAKES SENSE THAT IT SHOULD BE PASSED ON SINCE CHRIST CAME TO FREE US FROM SIN, AND HIS APOSTLES COULDN'T POSSIBLY REACH ALL TIMES AND PLACES.

SO, CAN YOU FORGIVE EVERY KIND OF SIN?
NOTHING IS BEYOND THE REACH OF GOD'S MERCY! I CAN FORGIVE ALL VENIAL AND MORTAL SINS!

WHAT'S THE DIFFERENCE?

THINK OF VENIAL SINS AS SMALL DETOURS ON THE ROAD TO HEAVEN...
THEY DEFLECT THE SOUL ON ITS PATH TO GOD, ITS END.
GOD

MORTAL SINS, ON THE OTHER HAND, ARE DEADLY--JUST AS THEIR NAME IMPLIES. IN THESE, A PERSON REJECTS GOD AS HIS END, BREAKS OFF HIS FRIENDSHIP WITH HIM AND KILLS THE DIVINE LIFE HE RECEIVED AT BAPTISM.

IN OTHER WORDS, MORTAL SIN CAUSES A SEPARATION FROM GOD THAT CAN LAST FOREVER IF WE DIE UNREPENTANT.

SO DO A NUMBER OF VENIAL SINS ADD UP TO A MORTAL SIN?

NO, EVEN A MILLION VENIAL SINS CAN'T EQUAL ONE MORTAL SIN! BUT THEY CAN PAVE THE WAY FOR ONE!
WHAT DO YOU MEAN?

WELL, IMAGINE THAT A SOUL IN A STATE OF GRACE IS LIKE A CLEAR WINDOW LETTING IN GOD'S GRACE AS SUNLIGHT...

VENIAL SINS WOULD BE LIKE DUST AND SOOT THAT STICK TO THE GLASS AND GRADUALLY LESSEN THE AMOUNT OF LIGHT COMING IN.

AS THE LIGHT OF GOD'S GRACE DIMINISHES, THE SOUL IS MORE PRONE TO COMMITTING GREATER SINS, EVEN MORTAL ONES!

AND CONFESSION "CLEANS THE WINDOW?"
EXACTLY!

HOW DO I KNOW IF I'VE COMMITTED A MORTAL SIN OR A VENIAL ONE?

VENIAL SINS ARE LESS SERIOUS, WHILE MORTAL SINS INVOLVE GRAVE MATTER THAT'S KNOWN AND FREELY CHOSEN.

GRAVE MATTER?? YOU MEAN, LIKE ROBBING CEMETERIES?

NO, GRAVE MATTER HAS LITTLE TO DO WITH GRAVES AND EVERYTHING TO DO WITH THE GRAVITY OF A SIN.
SO MURDER, ADULTERY, AND SKIPPING MASS ON SUNDAYS ARE ALL GRAVE MATTER.

If you were to commit one of them, knowing it to be a serious sin and choosing it freely, you would be guilty of a mortal sin.

Hang on! How can missing Mass on Sunday be as bad as committing murder!?

Well, murder is a serious sin against love of neighbor, and missing Mass is a serious sin against love of God.

It's hard to claim to love someone when you don't want to spend time with him!

But if I don't know that something is grave matter, then I can't commit a mortal sin, right?

Yes, but it's also our basic duty to know how to please God, and that knowledge is readily available...

Like someone who drives through a red traffic light, claiming he didn't know what it meant...

His ignorance doesn't help him, since he's expected to know traffic laws before getting on the road.
TICKET

I can see that.

What I don't see is why any sin should bother God in the first place!
What do you mean?

Well sins are done in time, and time moves on...
But God is outside of time and can't be hurt, so what's the big deal? What's past is past, right?

Sure, time moves on, but the effects of actual sin on a soul don't go away without God's grace.

Just as one can suffer the effects of wounds in one's body for years to come, so we can carry the burden of sins on our souls for years.

Healing those wounds is one of the effects of the grace received in Confession. Another one is strengthening the soul against falling into the same sins.

IF THAT'S THE CASE, THEN WHY DO PEOPLE GO TO CONFESSION AGAIN AND AGAIN? ONCE SHOULD BE ENOUGH!

IT *WOULD* BE ENOUGH IF WE WEREN'T SUCH WEAK, WOUNDED CREATURES WITH A TENDENCY TO SIN.

SO ONLY SAINTS DON'T NEED TO GO TO CONFESSION MORE THAN ONCE?

NO, EVEN SAINTS SIN. YET THEIR GREAT LOVE FOR GOD URGES THEM TO GO TO CONFESSION *MORE OFTEN* THAN THOSE WHO NEED IT MORE!

SO IF YOU WANT TO BE A SAINT AND LIVE IN GOD'S PEACE, I SUGGEST YOU IMITATE THEIR EXAMPLE!

I'LL THINK ABOUT IT.

WAS THAT THE LAST TIME YOU SAW HER?

NO, SHE RETURNED A FEW DAYS LATER FOR CONFESSION, DETERMINED TO START A NEW LIFE.

IN FACT, A YEAR OR TWO LATER, SHE FELT THE CALL TO RELIGIOUS LIFE AND ENDED UP JOINING A CONVENT OF NUNS.
SADLY, HER FATHER COULDN'T UNDERSTAND AND SHE HAD TO LEAVE HOME IN SECRET...

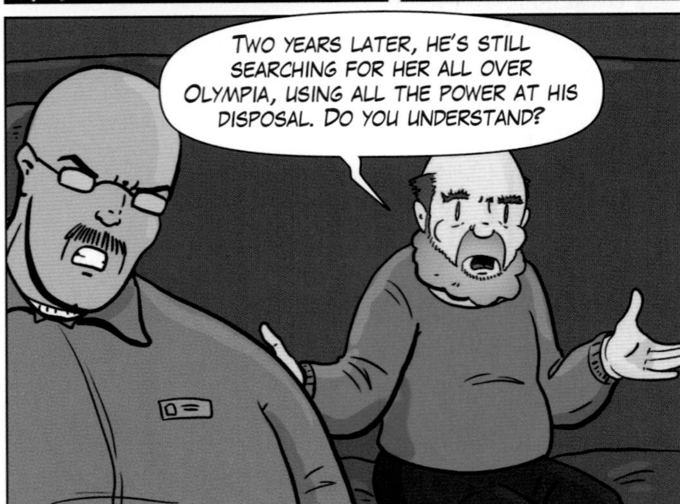
TWO YEARS LATER, HE'S STILL SEARCHING FOR HER ALL OVER OLYMPIA, USING ALL THE POWER AT HIS DISPOSAL. DO YOU UNDERSTAND?

SHE'S THE GOVERNOR'S DAUGHTER!
WHAT??

THE NEXT DAY...
CHAPTER 10
OPERATION FIRECAST

THUMP

Yesterday's meeting between Governor Alfonsi and Earth's financial board was a resounding success, ensuring the continued funding of Project Paradise.
PROJECT PARADISE
Later, the Governor spoke of their latest success...

We've got earth-like air density as well as temperatures that haven't been seen on this planet in billions of years!

...And this is just the beginning! Already the Amazonian Plain is being prepared for habitation by this week's end.

Meanwhile, in the cellar of the Pierced Pelican...
The Pierced Pelican

The Paradise Project is moving faster than we expected! They're planning to start moving people on Friday morning.

Great! Less attention on us!
Yes, but less attention on our broadcast too!

Hence we've decided to move the transmission date up.
Oh! Is everything ready?

The video's been ready for months, and our partners in the Underground Christian Churches were told of the change this morning...

They responded that they're ready to go whenever we give the word.

There are other underground churches??
Yes. When the new laws came in, the various denominations united under the Evangelical Pastor...

Unfortunately, Steve was captured a month ago. Though I hear his replacement is just as eager to spread the Good News.

Anyway, you'll find out firsthand when you meet Pastor Ezekiel on Friday.

Let's go over the plan...
Where and when are we supposed to meet this pastor and what do we do then?

The broadcast takes place at exactly 9:15 PM on Friday night, during Prime Time, when we can reach the most people.

At 8:45 PM, you're to pick up Pastor Ezekiel and a technician at the Larson Street Pad in Sector Two.

They'll hook up the transmitting equipment to your ship, and ride with you to an altitude of 124,000 feet...

Where they will broadcast *Firecast* at a quarter past nine.

After that, drop the Pastor and his man off at a quiet pad in Sector One and continue your work as usual.

What about the government? Can't they trace the signal back to our ship?

The whole broadcast will take one minute-- too short to trace, especially when they're not expecting it.

That may be, but there *will* be a reaction, and it's bound to make our lives more difficult...

Is it worth it?

Is the salvation of souls worth it?

Come on! We're broadcasting to people who have been brainwashed for years, and you think they're going to change their lives in 60 seconds??

IF I WERE JUDGING BY HUMAN STANDARDS, I'D AGREE WITH YOU!
BUT YOU'RE NOT SEEING THE MOST IMPORTANT PART, THE PART THAT MAKES THIS RISK REASONABLE.

THE COUNTLESS PRAYERS AND SACRIFICES THAT HAVE BEEN MADE FOR THESE PEOPLE!
THESE ARE OUR "SECRET WEAPONS" THAT BEG GOD TO OPEN THE HEARTS OF THE OLYMPIANS!

OTHERWISE, NEITHER A ONE-MINUTE NOR A 100-HOUR VIDEO CAN CONVERT A SINGLE SOUL...
...THERE'S JUST NO SUBSTITUTE FOR GOD'S GRACE!

SO WHY BOTHER BROADCASTING? JUST KEEP PRAYING AND SACRIFICING, AND GOD WILL TAKE CARE OF EVERYTHING!

AS I LIKE TO SAY, "PRAY AS THOUGH EVERYTHING DEPENDED ON GOD. WORK AS THOUGH EVERYTHING DEPENDED ON YOU."

GOD DOESN'T NEED ANYONE'S HELP, BUT HE FREELY CHOOSES TO MAKE USE OF HUMAN INSTRUMENTS TO BRING HIS GRACE TO OTHERS.

IT WAS SO IN THE INCARNATION, WHEN THE WORD OF GOD BECAME MAN THROUGH A WOMAN...

IT WAS SO WHEN CHRIST INSTITUTED THE SACRAMENTS, BRINGING GRACES TO OTHERS THROUGH MEN AND ELEMENTS LIKE WATER, OIL, AND WINE...

AND IT'S SO EVEN WHEN IT COMES TO TRANSMITTING GRACES TO ONE ANOTHER, WHETHER BY WORD, DEED, OR BROADCAST!

BUT SURELY HE COULD DO A BETTER JOB WITHOUT US!

SURE HE COULD! BUT AS OUR LOVING FATHER, HE SHARES HIS LIFE WITH US, GIVING US A CHANCE TO PARTICIPATE IN HIS WORK.

AND WHAT COULD BE MORE GOD-LIKE THAN BEING CHANNELS OF HIS GRACES TO OTHERS?
BESIDES, THIS MAY BE OUR LAST WINDOW OF OPPORTUNITY BEFORE THE OLYMPIANS ARE SCATTERED FAR AND WIDE.

SO WHAT DO YOU SAY? ARE YOU UP FOR SOME ADVENTURE?
SURE.
I GUESS.

The next day...
Look, Erc, we've got mail!
Chapter II: The Governor's Complaint

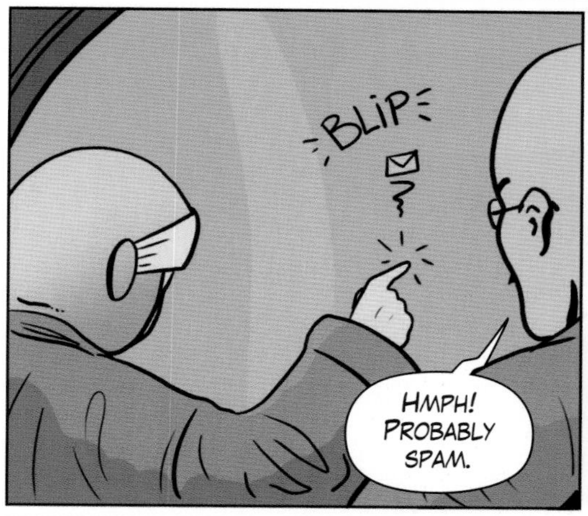
BLIP
Hmph! Probably spam.

Spam, spam, it's the best! Full of flavor, full of zest!

Full of flavor??
Full of zest!?

One more...
BLIP
Is any place safe from this stuff!?

Hello, captains Brendan and Erc. I'm calling on behalf of Governor Alfonsi...

The governor is inviting you to a private talk over drinks on Wednesday night at eight o'clock. Please confirm that you'll be there...

That's tonight!
Hey! Free drinks!
We look forward to seeing you then.

That evening...

THIS IS OUR FINEST MARTIAN BREW, RED RUST!

AND WHAT CAN I GET YOU, CAPTAIN?
SOME OF YOUR FINEST MARTIAN WATER, PLEASE, GOVERNOR.

CALL ME LOU.

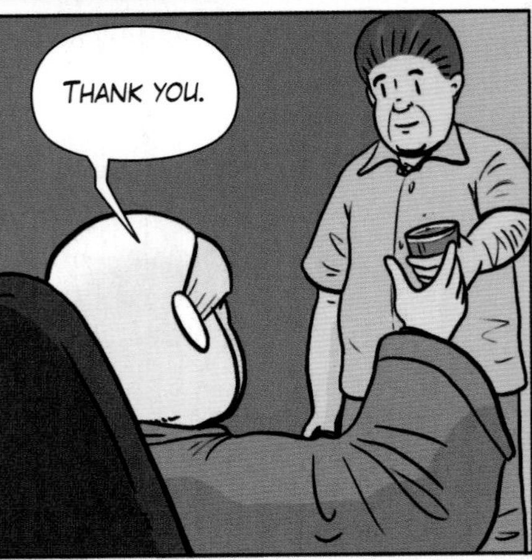
THANK YOU.

PERHAPS YOU'RE WONDERING WHY I CALLED FOR YOU.

I DOUBT YOU KNOW THIS, BUT I HAVE A DAUGHTER, AN ONLY CHILD.

I SENT HER TO THE BEST SCHOOLS AND PLANNED A PERFECT FUTURE FOR HER.
WE WERE VERY CLOSE... UNTIL A CERTAIN PRIEST CAME BETWEEN US.

HE MET WITH HER REGULARLY AND TURNED HER HEART AWAY FROM ME AND THE PROMISING LIFE I OFFERED HER.

I THOUGHT PRIESTS WERE BANNED FROM MARS.

THIS WAS BEFORE THE FREEDOM FROM RELIGION LAWS, AND IT CONVINCED ME OF THEIR NECESSITY.

NOBODY SHOULD HAVE TO GO THROUGH WHAT I'VE BEEN THROUGH!

ANYWAY, THANKS TO THAT PRIEST--FR. MICHAEL WAS WHAT HE WENT BY--SARAH LEFT HOME ONE NIGHT AND NEVER RETURNED.

WHAT, SHE VANISHED INTO THIN AIR?

SHE LEFT A NOTE. SOMETHING ABOUT GIVING HER LIFE TO GOD... WHATEVER THAT MEANS!

NATURALLY, I QUESTIONED FR. MICHAEL, BUT HE WOULDN'T SAY WHERE SHE'D GONE--ONLY THAT SHE WAS FOLLOWING A HIGHER CALL AND WOULD PRAY FOR ME.

I ENACTED THE FREEDOM LAWS SOON AFTER AND SENT POLICE TO ARREST HIM, BUT HE WAS GONE, HIDDEN BY FRIENDS NO DOUBT.

UM, WHAT DOES THIS HAVE TO DO WITH US?

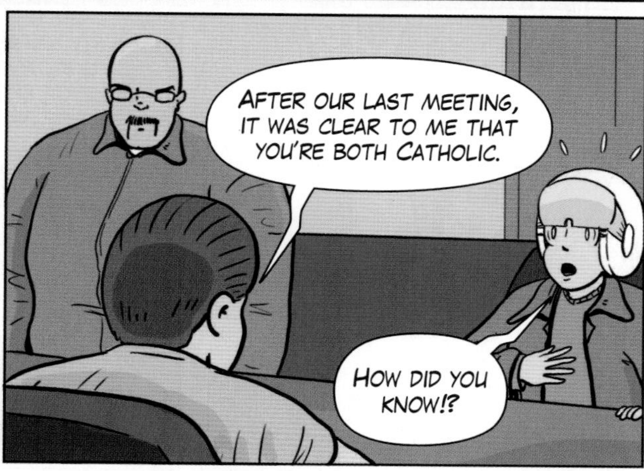
AFTER OUR LAST MEETING, IT WAS CLEAR TO ME THAT YOU'RE BOTH CATHOLIC.
HOW DID YOU KNOW!?

HEH, NO ONE IS MORE OBSESSED WITH SIN AND GUILT...

ANYWAY, I THOUGHT YOU MIGHT HAVE COME ACROSS THIS FR. MICHAEL, OR THAT HE MIGHT TRY TO CONTACT AND MANIPULATE YOU.

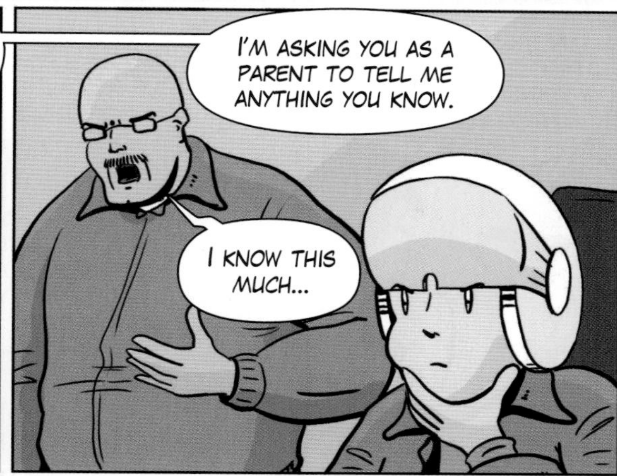
I'M ASKING YOU AS A PARENT TO TELL ME ANYTHING YOU KNOW.
I KNOW THIS MUCH...

YES...?

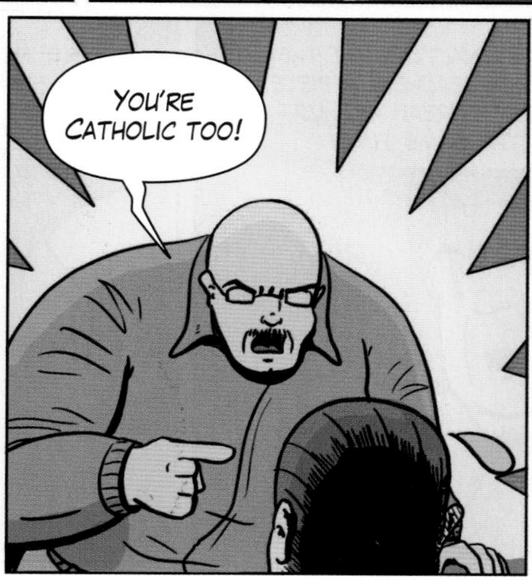
YOU'RE CATHOLIC TOO!

HA HA HA! I WAS CATHOLIC, BUT I OUTGREW IT IN COLLEGE.

DID YOU FIGURE THAT OUT ON YOUR OWN, OR DID SOMEONE HELP YOU?

Yes, my doubts began before my first communion...

When we learned about the Eucharist in our catechism class.

Now, I've come across many absurd ideas in religion, but that's the worst by far!
Why do you say that?

Where do I begin!?

First, you're expected to believe that a piece of bread isn't a piece of bread at all!
Oh no! It's the body of a man! And not *just* a man, but a *God-man!*

Talk about an insult to your intelligence!

Never mind the other contradictions involved, the whole thing is simply absurd!

Hey, God can do anything he wants! And it's by God's power that bread and wine become the body and blood of Jesus Christ.

But God can't make a contradiction not be a contradiction.
Huh?

I mean, even infinite power can't make something be true and not true at the same time in the same way.

And yet that's *exactly* what the Catholic Church teaches! A piece of bread is both bread and *not* bread at the same time!

But not in the same way!
What??

If you put the same outfit on all three their substance wouldn't change a bit, though they might look the same.

CHRIST IS IN HEAVEN IN HIS RESURRECTED BODY...

AND HE'S ALSO IN THE HOST WITH HIS RESURRECTED BODY, BUT IN A DIFFERENT MODE... A *SACRAMENTAL* ONE!

WHAT'S THAT FANCY LANGUAGE SUPPOSED TO MEAN?

IMAGINE A MILLION MIRRORS REFLECTING THE SUN...

IF YOU ADDED A MILLION MORE MIRRORS, IT WOULDN'T TAKE ANYTHING AWAY FROM THE SUN, BUT IT WOULD MULTIPLY ITS IMAGE.

IT'S A LITTLE LIKE THAT WITH THE EUCHARIST, EXCEPT THAT THE MIRRORS AND THE SUN WOULD HAVE THE SAME SUBSTANCE, THOUGH DIFFERENT ACCIDENTS.

SOUNDS LIKE NONSENSE TO ME! ANYWAY, GIVE ME A CALL IF YOU COME ACROSS THIS FR. MICHAEL.
NOW IF YOU'LL EXCUSE ME, I HAVE OTHER MATTERS TO LOOK INTO... I TRUST YOU KNOW YOUR WAY OUT.

KERR!
BLIP

YES, GOVERNOR?

IT'S AS WE SUSPECTED-- THEY'RE CATHOLIC.
PUT A WATCH ON THEM ASAP, BUT KEEP YOUR DISTANCE...

I THINK WE CAN EXPECT A BIG CATCH SOON!

CHAPTER 12:
A SACRAMENT FOR THE SICK

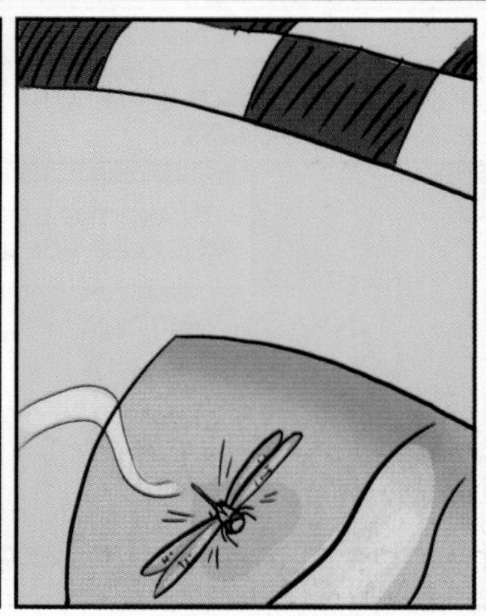

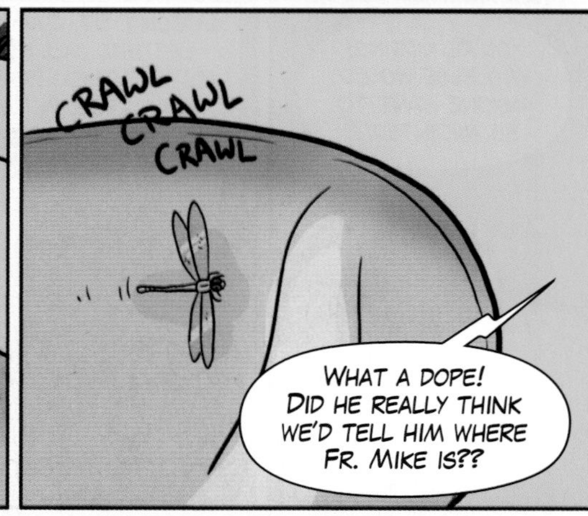
CRAWL CRAWL CRAWL
WHAT A DOPE! DID HE REALLY THINK WE'D TELL HIM WHERE FR. MIKE IS??

SPEAKING OF WHOM, WE'D BETTER HURRY UP IF WE WANT TO MEET HIM ON TIME.

SOON...
OPEN

WHERE TO, FATHER?
THE HERGE STREET HOSPITAL.

AREN'T YOU FEELING WELL?

I'M FINE, IT'S ONE OF MY PARISHIONERS WHO'S IN BAD SHAPE. SOUNDS LIKE HE WON'T LIVE LONG!

So what are you going to do? Heal him?
Anoint him! What happens after that is up to God.

But he *could* get better, right? The Sacrament of Anointing could cure him, couldn't it?

Sure it could! Plenty of people get better after an Anointing, but that's not the main reason Christ gave us this sacrament.

You're kidding! Why else would anyone want to be anointed!?

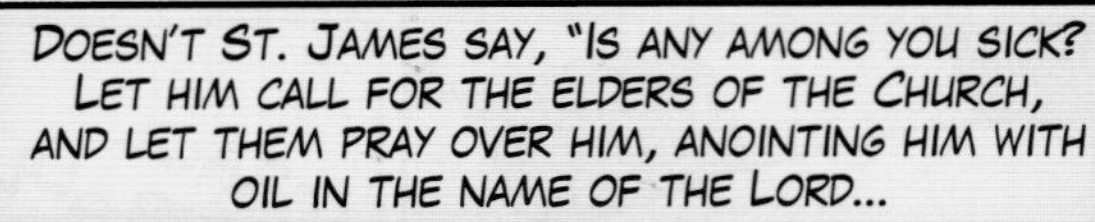
Doesn't St. James say, "Is any among you sick? Let him call for the elders of the Church, and let them pray over him, anointing him with oil in the name of the Lord...

"...and the Lord will raise him up"?
*Jas 5:14-15

Why get a man's hopes up only to dash them to pieces??

There's more to a man's life than bodily health! Plenty of good can come from illness and the knowledge that death is near.

For God "disciplines us for our good, that we may share his holiness."*
*Heb 12:10

So Anointing of the Sick primarily *strengthens* us in suffering, uniting our sufferings to those of Christ.

But it also has power to take away sins if a person isn't able to confess. And if it's God's will, it can even restore one's health.

But if it's God's will that the person dies, then Anointing, followed by Viaticum, prepares him for the passage from this life to the next.

In fact, it's not unreasonable to say that Anointing can shorten or even eliminate one's time in Purgatory!

What's this "Viaticum" thing?

It's the last Holy Communion a Catholic receives, during the Last Rites, which consoles and sanctifies him before meeting Christ face to face.

The word comes from the Latin, meaning "food for a journey"...

I thought the sacrament of Anointing is the same thing as Last Rites.

Last Rites *include* the Anointing of the Sick, but they assume that the person is dying, hence the name.

By them, a person is prepared for death by Confession, Anointing, and Viaticum, followed by a special blessing.

On the other hand, anyone who is seriously ill or feeble or in danger of death from sickness or old age, may receive the Anointing of the Sick.
Cough
Cough

So the man you're visiting is going to get the Last Rites, then?
Uh-huh.

Does that mean you've got Jesus in the Eucharist with you right now?

Well how else am I going to bring him to this poor soul?
Tap
Tap

But aren't you afraid something might happen to it? After all, the hospital is a public place...

I'm going in disguise. Nobody will suspect who I am or what I'm doing there.
But the governor is looking for you!
Tell me something I don't know.

I mean, the governor was just asking about you last night!

LISTEN PADRE, YOU DON'T HAVE TO GO. NOBODY WILL BLAME YOU IF YOU SKIP THIS SICK CALL.
NOBODY?

WHEN THE NEW LAWS CAME IN, I THOUGHT IT WOULD BE A MATTER OF HOURS BEFORE I WAS CAUGHT.

BUT I COULDN'T STAND WAITING TO BE PICKED UP, SO I WENT ABOUT DOING AS MUCH GOOD AS POSSIBLE, TAKING THE NECESSARY PRECAUTIONS, OF COURSE.

EACH MORNING I FEARED WOULD BE MY LAST, BUT IT FINALLY DAWNED ON ME THAT I'M HERE BECAUSE GOD WILLS IT, AND I'LL ONLY LEAVE WHEN AND HOW HE WILLS IT.

IN THE MEANTIME, MY JOB IS TO STRENGTHEN THE WEAK AND CONFIRM THE STRONG!
BUT, FATHER, WHAT ABOUT *FIRECAST*? NOW'S NOT THE TIME TO TAKE RISKS!

TRUST IN THE LORD, AND HE'LL TAKE CARE OF YOU.

I'LL SEE YOU HERE IN AN HOUR!

:CLICK:
:CLICK:

GOOD! JUST ENOUGH TIME TO GRAB SOME BREAKFAST!

The Golden Mug
CHAPTER 13:
THE MYSTERY OF MARRIAGE

I DON'T KNOW... THEY'RE ALL CUTE, BUT I'M NOT SURE ANY OF THEM REALLY FIT.
HOW ABOUT SOME OF OUR OLDER-LOOKING MODELS?

KEEP IN MIND THAT WE CAN MIX AND MATCH HEADS...

DID I MENTION THAT WE HAVE DOZENS OF HAIR COLORS TO CHOOSE FROM?
OOOH! THAT'S WHAT I WANT!

WHAT?
MAKE ME ONE LIKE HIM!

HELLO!
CAN I HELP YOU?

HI, I'M ROB FROM THE ROBOCO CORPORATION.

IS THIS YOUR CHILD?
NO!

I'M NOT A CHILD!
AH...

WELL, I HAVE A DEAL FOR YOU! WHAT'S YOUR NAME?
PAT PAT PAT
BRENDAN.

LISTEN, BRENDAN, HOW WOULD YOU LIKE TO BE THE FACE OF THE NEXT GENERATION OF ROBOKIDS?

WHAT??

THINK OF THE GOOD YOU COULD DO FOR PEOPLE, LIKE KATE, WHO WANT TO HAVE KIDS WITHOUT ANY INCONVENIENCE!
YOUR HELP IS MUCH APPRECIATED!

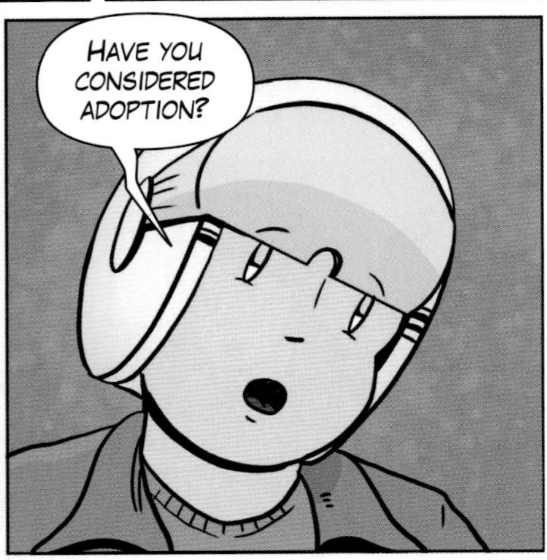
HAVE YOU CONSIDERED ADOPTION?

TOO MANY HASSLES, AND IT DOESN'T SOLVE THE BASIC PROBLEM THAT COMES WITH REAL CHILDREN...
WHICH IS...?

THE ENDLESS CLEANUP, THE FRUSTRATIONS, FEARS, AND SETBACKS THAT COME WITH PARENTING!

WHO IN HER RIGHT MIND WOULD INFLICT SUCH A LIFE ON HERSELF!?

AT ROBOCO, WE PUT A LOT OF TIME AND ENERGY INTO SOLVING THIS PROBLEM AND CAME UP WITH ROBOKIDS--"GUARANTEED CUTENESS THAT LASTS A LIFETIME!"

THEY'RE PROGRAMMED WITH HUMAN EMOTIONS AND SKILLS THAT RANGE FROM COOKING TO SATELLITE REPAIR!

SO FAR WE ONLY HAVE A DOZEN MODELS TO CHOOSE FROM, BUT THE POSSIBILITIES ARE GROWING!

For instance, thanks to the new human-droid marriage laws, we're seeing a rise in sales of RoboCo *Perfect Partners*.

Now the most natural thing in the world is for these couples to complete their perfect family with a *RoboKid!*

Perfect family...?

BOING

MMMMM
MMMM

Hmph! Sounds like a perfect *nightmare!*

So what do you say? This could be your lucky break.

It sounds to me like you don't understand the purpose and nature of marriage!

What do you mean!?
I mean that marriage is between a man and a woman, for life, and children are its fruit and purpose!

Ha ha ha! Come on! Marriage is an *option*, and like any option, it's chosen for its advantages!

In fact, surveys show that most people decide to forego marriage altogether and either live together as long as it's convenient, or buy a *Perfect Partner* from us.

That may be, but laws and surveys can't change the nature of marriage any more than they can change the nature of gravity.

...Only the one who *invented* marriage can change it!

If you give me his name and address, I'll see about sending him a proposal...
GOD!

Oh.

I see you two are religious types...
Let me just say that I've tried being married to a man and it was far from perfect.
Sorry to hear that.

Sure, it began full of love...

We got married a week after we met, and I had the joy of riding down Main Street on a mechanical elephant.

It was the happiest day of my life!

How long did it last?
It was all too short! Barely half an hour before the elephant reached the wedding hall!

I mean the marriage.
Oh... Almost a month.

But we really loved each other! At least at first. Isn't that enough??

It's a good start, but it's not the whole of marriage...

Marriage is a lifelong commitment of two people to each other, which means loving even when you don't feel love.

How can you love without *feeling* love? Isn't love a feeling??

Well, there *is* a feeling of love, but that's not enough for a good marriage.
For that you need a more stable and spiritual love, one you can *choose* with your will!

Never heard of it.

Sure you have!

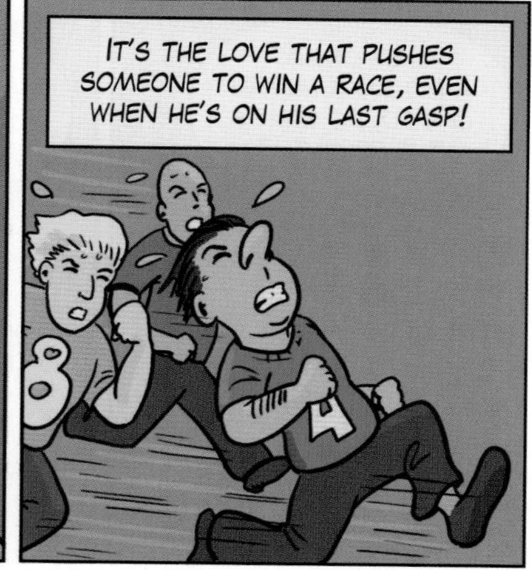
It's the love that pushes someone to win a race, even when he's on his last gasp!

It's the love that keeps you in the kitchen, even when it's 110 degrees inside!

In other words, a love that leads you to sacrifice yourself for the beloved.
That's what I was getting at!

That's all very romantic, but it just doesn't fit reality.

Sure, there are dogs who faithfully wait *years* for their master to come home...
DOG

And men who willingly sacrifice their lives to save their fellow soldiers...

But to live with the same person for 10, 15, or even 30 years, much less a lifetime, demands a heroism beyond mortal men!

Now, at RoboCo we're attuned to the needs of common men and women. That's why we developed the *Perfect Partner*--our top-selling line of personal droids!

Our *Perfect Partner* with its Lifelong Mate plan allows users to swap the head, body, and personality of their spouse on any given day!
Sheer genius!

You can call it whatever you want, but marrying a robot with gizmos is not a marriage!

He's right, you can't have a marriage without a man and a woman.

THEY CAN DO ANYTHING A HUMAN CAN DO, SO WHAT'S THE PROBLEM?

THEY CAN'T LOVE LIKE HUMANS... THEY CAN'T HAVE KIDS LIKE HUMANS...

COME ON! WHY DEFINE MARRIAGE BY CHILDREN?? PLENTY OF PEOPLE ARE MARRIED AND DON'T HAVE KIDS!

TELL ME, WHAT'S THE AVERAGE LIFESPAN OF ONE OF YOUR DROIDS?

OH, AT LEAST A HUNDRED YEARS! THOUGH WITH PROPER MAINTENANCE YOU PROBABLY COULD GET ANOTHER 25 OUT OF THEM!

AND HOW MANY HUMANS DO YOU SUPPOSE WILL LIVE THAT LONG?
HM, PROBABLY NOT TOO MANY...

SO IF THIS SOCIETY DOESN'T HAVE PLENTY OF BABIES, WHAT WILL IT LOOK LIKE IN ANOTHER CENTURY?

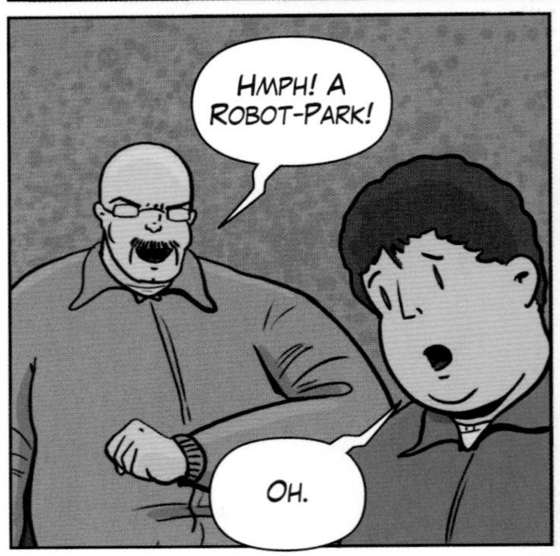
HMPH! A ROBOT-PARK!
OH.

BUT DO YOU REALLY THINK PEOPLE WOULD BE HAPPIER WITH IMPERFECT PARTNERS AND ALL THE MESS AND STRESS THAT COMES WITH BABIES?

IT DEPENDS ON WHAT YOU MEAN BY "HAPPIER"...

IF YOU MEAN A HAPPINESS THAT'S BASED ON SELF-LOVE AND PLEASURE, THEN NO, I DON'T THINK ANYONE WOULD BE HAPPIER RAISING A FAMILY...

BUT IF YOU MEAN A DEEP HAPPINESS THAT COMES FROM KNOWING TRUE LOVE AND OUR PURPOSE IN LIFE, THEN THERE'S NO DOUBT ABOUT THE BETTER CHOICE!

AFTER ALL, MARRIAGE IS MEANT TO BE A SCHOOL OF LOVE, AIMED AT HELPING MEN AND WOMEN FLOURISH.
School of Marriage
Apply Today!
Learn How to:
-Love
-Give
-Forgive

HEY, SOMETHING WRONG?

I CAN'T BELIEVE I'VE BEEN WORKING SO HARD AT DESTROYING MY OWN COMPANY...

EXCUSE ME...

BUT MARRIAGE IS SO HARD!

GOD KNOWS THAT, WHICH IS WHY HE GIVES COUPLES THE GRACES THEY NEED IN THE SACRAMENT OF MATRIMONY.

GREAT! WHERE DO I SIGN UP??

WELL, YOU NEED TO BE A BAPTIZED CHRISTIAN TO RECEIVE THE GRACES OF THE SACRAMENTS.
OH.

I'LL, AH, THINK ABOUT IT AND GET BACK TO YOU.
HEY! WE SHOULD GET GOING...

YOU MAKE IT SOUND LIKE THE SACRAMENT MAKES MARRIAGE EASY!

WELL, IT GIVES GRACES TO HELP THE COUPLE STAY FAITHFUL TO EACH OTHER, RAISE AND EDUCATE THEIR CHILDREN, AND GROW IN HOLINESS...
AND THAT'S NO SMALL THING!

BESIDES, IT MAKES VISIBLE THE LOVE OF CHRIST FOR HIS CHURCH-- "A PROFOUND MYSTERY" AS ST. PAUL SAYS.*

*EPH 5:32

THAT IS ONE REASON WHY A VALID, SACRAMENTAL MARRIAGE IS FOR LIFE... CHRIST CAN NEVER SEPARATE HIMSELF FROM THE CHURCH WHICH HAS BECOME ONE BODY WITH HIM!
MultiP
RETURNS

THIS IS AN URGENT NEWS BROADCAST...
ALER
HUH?

A DUST STORM IS DEVELOPING IN THE ARABIA TERRA REGION, PUTTING ALL COLONIZATION EFFORTS ON HOLD.

WOO HOO!
GIVEN THE CURRENT AIR DENSITY, THIS STORM WILL BE THE WORST IN MARTIAN HISTORY.
MEGA STORM
HENCE ALL ARE ADVISED TO STAY INSIDE THE LIMITS OF OLYMPIA.

ALSO JUST IN--POLICE SHOT THE CRIMINAL, CATHOLIC PRIEST, MICHAEL HALEY, AS HE ATTEMPTED TO ESCAPE...
GASP!

DRONES CAPTURED THIS FOOTAGE EARLIER TODAY.

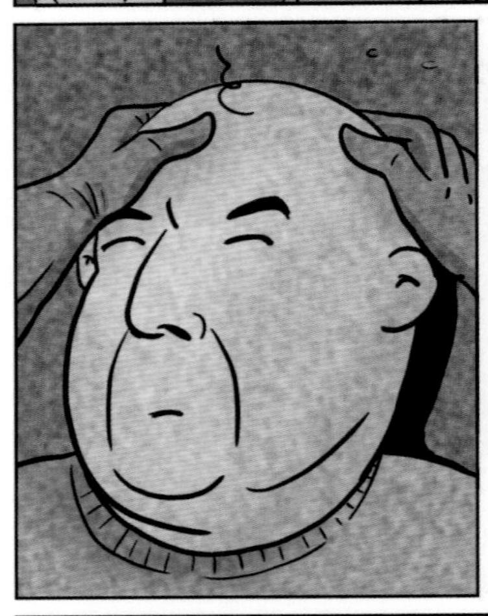

NO!

NO!!

BRENDAN! WAIT!

CHAPTER 14:
A DEEPENING DARKNESS

PANT PANT YOU COULD HAVE WAITED FOR ME!

LOOK, I KNOW HOW YOU FEEL. IT WAS A SURPRISE FOR ME TOO!

WHO COULD HAVE GUESSED WHERE FR. MIKE WOULD BE TODAY, ESPECIALLY WITH THE GETUP HE HAD ON?

THAT'S JUST IT, ERC, NOBODY COULD HAVE GUESSED!

WHAT?! YOU THINK THERE'S A SPY IN THE UNDERGROUND??

I don't know, but if you figure he's been wanted all these years and nobody caught him till we came along, I'd say we're the most probable suspects.

Come on! That's ridiculous!

You know I didn't turn him in, and I know you didn't turn him in...

Yes, but remember that night at the Governor's palace? He guessed we were Catholic.

So what? You think it's connected??
It's too coincidental!

Well, if we're tagged, we should do the Underground a favor and go back to Earth.
NO!

Hey, this planet's been nothing but trouble since we got here, and now you want to stay??

We promised to fly *Firecast*! They need us!

That was back when Fr. Mike was alive! Who knows what the plan is now?

He told us to trust in God. We can ask Deacon Alex if the whole thing's off.

Fine.

LATER...

YOU'RE LOOKING FOR ALEX, AREN'T YOU?
YES!

HE THOUGHT YOU MIGHT SHOW UP HERE AFTER YOU SAW THE NEWS...

HE WANTED ME TO TELL YOU THAT NOTHING'S CHANGED AND BE EXTRA CAREFUL.

THANKS!

MAY FR. MIKE'S PRAYERS GO WITH YOU!

THAT NIGHT...

ZZZZZ

WHAT'S GOING ON??

WHERE'S ALL THIS DARKNESS COMING FROM??
GASP!
AAAAAAHHHHHH!!
HUH?
IT'S TIME!
BEEP
BEEP
BEEP

Later that night...
Chapter 15:
A Mysterious Priesthood

I hope someone's waiting for us down there.
We'll find out in a minute!

You!
You're Pastor Ezekiel??

At your service!
And this is Nathan, our tech wizard.
Hi.

Sorry about Mike. I understand he was a devoted pastor... Mars could use more like him.
Thanks.

I'LL TELL YOU WHAT MARS COULD USE-- SOMEONE TO BRING IT TO ITS *KNEES!*

I THOUGHT THAT'S WHAT THIS *FIRECAST* THING IS ALL ABOUT!
NO YOU, YOU... *APE!* THAT'S NOT WHAT I MEANT AT ALL!

NATHAN!

NATHAN THINKS WE'RE BEING TOO SOFT WITH THESE PEOPLE.

THE ONLY THING THAT'S GOING TO CHANGE THEIR HEARTS IS THE REAL AND IMMEDIATE THREAT OF *TOTAL ANNIHILATION!*

WAS THAT WHAT CHRIST TAUGHT HIS DISCIPLES?
DESPERATE TIMES CALL FOR DESPERATE MEASURES...

PEOPLE DON'T GO FOR "LOVE YOUR ENEMIES" ANYMORE!

DID THEY EVER?

SO WHAT ARE YOUR PEOPLE DOING ABOUT REPLACING MIKE?

DEACON ALEX IS IN CHARGE RIGHT NOW, BUT WE NEED ANOTHER PRIEST TO TAKE FATHER'S PLACE.

WHY? ISN'T ALEX A GOOD LEADER?

HE IS, BUT HE'S NOT A *PRIEST!*

?
?

I MEAN HE CAN'T OFFER THE MASS OR GIVE US MOST OF THE SACRAMENTS!

I THOUGHT WE WERE ALL PRIESTS! DOESN'T PETER CALL US "A ROYAL PRIESTHOOD"?*
*1 PET 2:9

THAT'S TRUE, BUT ST. PETER IS REFERRING TO OUR COMMON PRIESTHOOD IN CHRIST, THE PERFECT PRIEST.
IT'S NOT THE SAME AS BEING A PRIEST.

WHAT'S THE DIFFERENCE?

FOR ONE THING, YOU CALL A PRIEST "FATHER."

UM, EVERYONE RECEIVES THE COMMON PRIESTHOOD BY BAPTISM AND CONFIRMATION.*
* CCC 1546

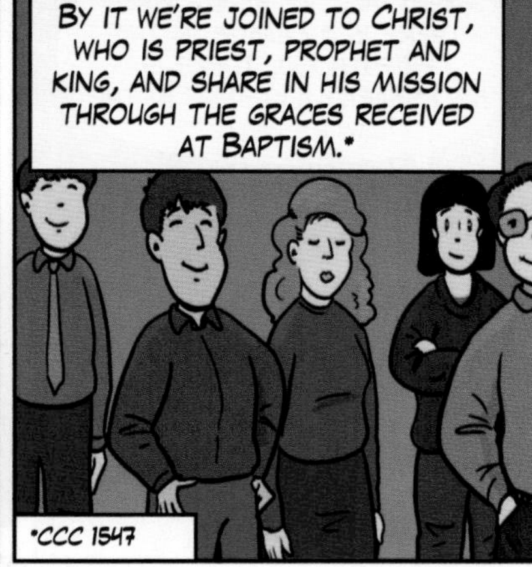
BY IT WE'RE JOINED TO CHRIST, WHO IS PRIEST, PROPHET AND KING, AND SHARE IN HIS MISSION THROUGH THE GRACES RECEIVED AT BAPTISM.*
*CCC 1547

BUT ORDAINED PRIESTS BUILD UP AND LEAD THE CHURCH, SERVING GOD'S PEOPLE AND ACTING AS INSTRUMENTS OF CHRIST TO DEVELOP THOSE GRACES.*
*CCC 1547

THAT'S INTERESTING, BUT WITH ALL DUE RESPECT, THERE'S NOTHING ABOUT AN ORDAINED PRIESTHOOD IN THE NEW TESTAMENT.
YEAH, BECAUSE CHRIST *ABOLISHED* THE PRIESTHOOD!

LIKE IT SAYS IN HEBREWS, "HE HOLDS HIS PRIESTHOOD PERMANENTLY, BECAUSE HE CONTINUES FOR EVER."*
*HEB 7:24

No need for other priests when Christ is a priest *forever!*

True, Christ IS a priest forever, and his priesthood is perfect, but he also chooses certain men to share in this priesthood.

Think of the Israelites, whom God called "a kingdom of priests and a holy nation."*
*Exod 19:6

Yet this didn't prevent him from also setting apart Aaron and his sons as priests to serve at his altar.*
*Exod 28:1

Since Christians are just as much God's chosen people, there's no reason why there can't be a ministerial AND a common priesthood in the New Testament too!

Otherwise, why does the letter to the Hebrews speak about "an altar from which those who serve the tent have no right to eat" if there are no priests to serve at that altar?*
*Heb 13:10

Well, I don't see why you need priests when Christ fulfilled the Old Covenant by his sacrifice on the cross.

After all, we read, "When there is a change in the priesthood, there is necessarily a change in the law as well."*
*Heb 7:12

And, "He has no need, like those high priests, to offer sacrifices daily ... he did this once for all when he offered up himself."*
*Heb 7:27

So the Old Law with its priestly sacrifices is abolished, and the New Law with one Priest and his perfect sacrifice takes its place.
Anything more is superfluous!

If Christ thought it was superfluous, then why did he bother to ordain priests??

What do you mean?

I mean, if Jesus didn't think we needed priests anymore, then why did he tell his apostles to do priestly things, like offer sacrifices and forgive sins?*
These aren't things that *any* Christian can do!
*Luke 22:19, John 20:23

WHAT SACRIFICE COULD POSSIBLY TAKE THE PLACE OF THE ONE, PERFECT SACRIFICE OF CHRIST ON THE CROSS, AND WHO WOULD DARE OFFER IT??

ONLY CHRIST CAN MAKE THAT OFFERING BECAUSE ONLY HE IS THE PERFECT PRIEST!

THAT'S WHAT I'M SAYING! THERE'S NO *NEED* FOR A PRIESTHOOD ANYMORE!

AS LONG AS THERE'S A NEED FOR SACRIFICE, THERE'S A NEED FOR PRIESTS, BECAUSE MAN HAS ALWAYS WORSHIPED GOD WITH SACRIFICE!

THE ONLY CHANGE AFTER CHRIST WAS FROM AN IMPERFECT TO A PERFECT SACRIFICE, OFFERED THROUGHOUT THE WORLD AS GOD PREDICTED THROUGH THE PROPHET MALACHI...
"FOR FROM THE RISING OF THE SUN TO ITS SETTING MY NAME IS GREAT AMONG THE NATIONS, AND IN EVERY PLACE INCENSE IS OFFERED TO MY NAME, AND A PURE OFFERING".*
*MAL 1:11 N.B. IN THE OLD COVENANT, SACRIFICES COULD ONLY BE OFFERED IN ONE PLACE: HIS TEMPLE.

SO IT'S CHRIST WHO SHARES HIS PRIESTHOOD WITH ORDAINED MEN SO THEY CAN OFFER HIS PURE AND PERFECT SACRIFICE FOR SOULS IN THE MASS.

YOU MEAN THEY RE-SACRIFICE CHRIST, AS THOUGH HIS OFFERING ON CALVARY WASN'T GOOD ENOUGH!!

NO, NO THAT'S NOT IT AT ALL!

IN THE SACRIFICE OF THE MASS, THE PRIEST ACTING ON CHRIST'S BEHALF MAKES PRESENT ON THE ALTAR THE SAME OFFERING OF OUR LORD, JESUS CHRIST, ON CALVARY.
IT'S NOT *ANOTHER* SACRIFICE BUT THAT SAME, PERFECT ONE OFFERED BY JESUS TO HIS FATHER, FOR US ALL.

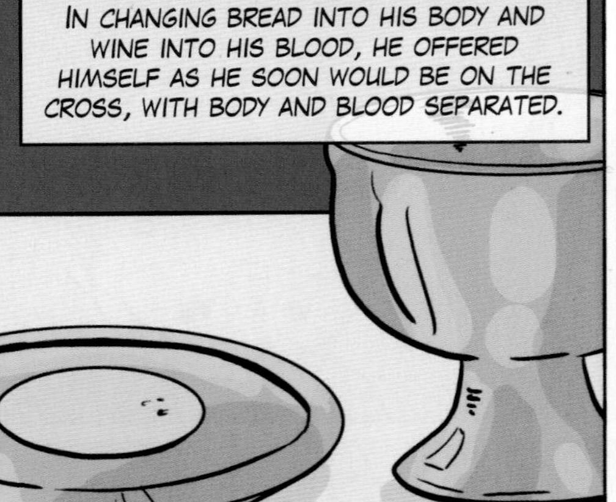

*Luke 22:19

*1 Cor 11:26

*Cf. Heb 6:20

*Gen 14:18

ALSO, "THE LORD HAS SWORN AND WILL NOT CHANGE HIS MIND, "YOU ARE A PRIEST FOR EVER AFTER THE ORDER OF MELCHIZEDEK."*
*PS 110:4

BUT AS THE LETTER TO THE HEBREWS SAYS, A PRIEST IS ONE WHO HAS SOMETHING TO OFFER, AND CHRIST OFFERS HIMSELF IN THE FORM OF BREAD AND WINE.*
*HEB 8:3

SO HOW CAN HE OFFER THIS SACRIFICE "FOREVER" EXCEPT THROUGH AN ORDAINED PRIESTHOOD ON EARTH?

YEAH! YOU WON'T FIND ANY BREAD AND WINE IN HEAVEN!

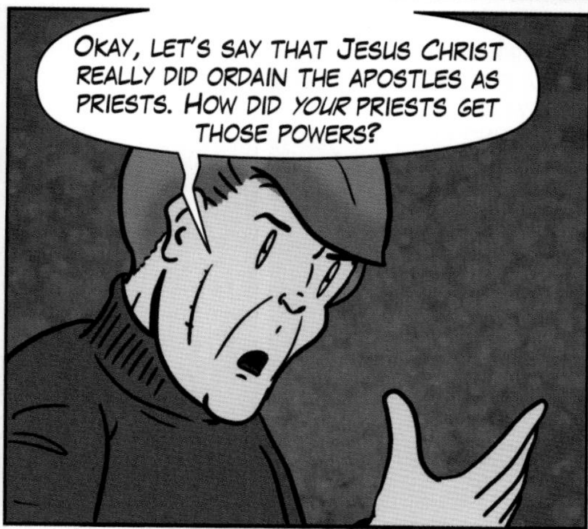
OKAY, LET'S SAY THAT JESUS CHRIST REALLY DID ORDAIN THE APOSTLES AS PRIESTS. HOW DID YOUR PRIESTS GET THOSE POWERS?

BY THE LAYING ON OF HANDS FROM A VALIDLY ORDAINED BISHOP.*
*CF. 2 TIM 1:6

IN FACT, EVERY CATHOLIC* BISHOP CAN TRACE HIS ORDINATION TO ONE OF THE APOSTLES, WHO RECEIVED THEIR SHARE IN THE PRIESTHOOD OF JESUS CHRIST!
*AND ORTHODOX

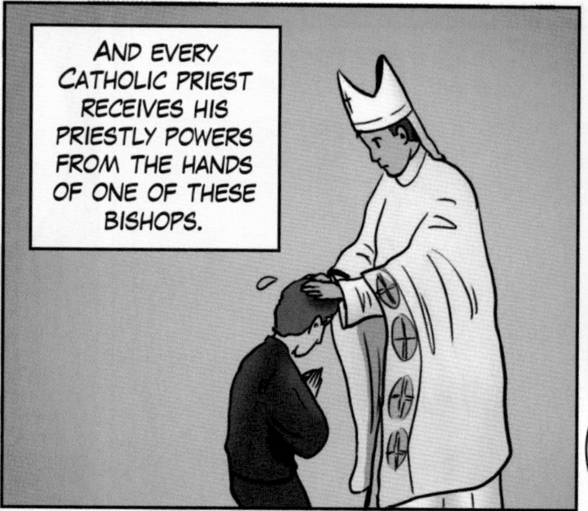
AND EVERY CATHOLIC PRIEST RECEIVES HIS PRIESTLY POWERS FROM THE HANDS OF ONE OF THESE BISHOPS.

IT'S REALLY AMAZING, IF YOU THINK ABOUT IT!

IT'S SCANDALOUS, IF YOU ASK ME!

WHY'S THAT??

HOW CAN CHRIST SHARE HIS POWER WITH MEN??
MAYBE SOME OF THEM ARE SAINTLY, BUT MOST ARE AS SINFUL AS THE REST OF US!

THEY DO GET SPECIAL GRACES TO HELP THEM...

BUT YOU CAN'T DENY THAT NOT ALL YOUR PRIESTS AND BISHOPS HAVE LIVED UP TO THOSE GRACES!
TRUE...

AND THEN THEY HAVE THE NERVE TO PRETEND TO ABSOLVE OTHER PEOPLE OF THEIR SINS!!

THAT'S LIKE GETTING YOUR WINDOWS CLEANED WITH A GREASY RAG!

NO, IT'S LIKE GETTING HEALED BY A SICK DOCTOR OR GETTING WATER FROM AN UNDERGROUND PIPE.

HUH??

THE PRIEST IS ONLY AN INSTRUMENT, A CHANNEL OF GOD'S GRACES MADE PRESENT IN THE SACRAMENTS.

SO, JUST AS A SICK DOCTOR DOESN'T LOSE HIS ABILITY TO HEAL...

OR A PIPE DOESN'T LOSE ITS CAPACITY TO DIRECT WATER, NO MATTER WHAT FILTH SURROUNDS IT, A PRIEST OR BISHOP IN SIN CAN STILL GIVE OTHERS GOD'S GRACE.

THE SACRAMENTS TRANSMIT GRACE REGARDLESS OF THE MINISTER'S STATE OF SOUL...
BEEP! BEEP! BEEP!

SPEAKING OF TRANSMITTING...
IT'S TIME!

CHAPTER 16:
CASTING FIRE IN THE NIGHT
I TOLD YOU NUMBSKULLS NOT TO TOUCH ANYTHING TILL I GOT BACK!

BLIP

CLICK
CLICK
CLICK

HEY YOU!
HUH?
YES, YOU!

EVER FEEL LIKE THERE'S SOMETHING MISSING IN YOUR LIFE?

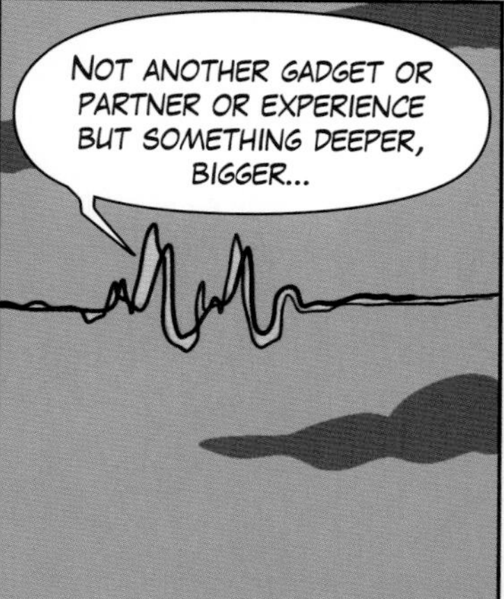
NOT ANOTHER GADGET OR PARTNER OR EXPERIENCE BUT SOMETHING DEEPER, BIGGER...

A GNAWING FEELING THAT THERE'S GOT TO BE MORE, MUCH MORE TO LIFE?
THE GOOD NEWS IS THAT IT DOES EXIST AND YOU CAN GET IT!

INTERESTED? TAKE THE FIRST STEP AND TURN TO GOD, ASKING FOR A NEW LIFE.

HEY, HE'S THE ONE WHO GAVE YOU YOUR LIFE IN THE FIRST PLACE AND HE LOVES YOU BEYOND YOUR WILDEST DREAMS!

LOOK AT JESUS CHRIST, GOD'S LOVE MADE PLAIN BEFORE YOUR EYES, AND THE HOPE HE HOLDS OUT TO YOU.

Yes, to YOU! And isn't that what you're really after? A trustworthy hope?
Hope in this life and in the next. A hope that doesn't fall through or disappoint.

Look, you've tried everything else, so why not try this?
...It might change your life forever.

Open your hearts now, See what's inside. Don't be afraid, of what you may find.
Turn to your Maker, turn and repent, Discover God's mercy; begin your ascent.
Uni-gas

Turn to Christ Jesus, rest in his love. Then you'll find true joy that comes from above.

KERR!

BLIP
Yes sir?
Did you see that??
What?

The Christians are flooding Mars with propaganda!

We have to fight back before anyone falls for their lies!
Yes sir.

Arrange a Press Conference for me ASAP and arrest those Catholic pilots. They're bound to know something about this.
Will do.
And Kerr?

Yes?

Never talk to me with that silly thing on your head!

Meanwhile...

I'd suggest we all disappear for a while until the government's reaction cools off.

Maybe it's time we quit and went back home before we... before things go bad for us too.

You mean before we end up like Fr. Mike?
Mm hm.

!
Sure, go back to Earth and save yourselves!

Live nice, comfortable lives, full of a Christian charity that doesn't cost anything!

Hey, we promised to fly *Firecast* and we did! Our part is done!

Besides, what more can we do around here with Fr. Mike dead and gone?

Hmph! Bunch of gullible nitwits!

Why do you say that??

WHAT MAKES YOU THINK YOUR FATHER MIKE IS DEAD??

HOW COULD HE NOT BE!?
COME ON! WE ALL SAW HIM GET BLASTED ON TV!

DID IT EVER OCCUR TO YOU THAT NOT EVERY BLAST IS MEANT TO BE LETHAL??

WAKE UP!

IT'S NO SECRET THAT THE GOVERNOR IS SEARCHING FOR HIS DAUGHTER AND THAT MIKE KNOWS WHERE SHE IS...
HE'D BE OUT OF HIS MIND TO HAVE YOUR PRIEST SHOT AND KILLED BEFORE PUMPING HIM FOR INFORMATION!

YOU REALLY THINK SO??

I THINK NATHAN'S ON TO SOMETHING.

BUT WHY DIDN'T THE NEWS JUST SAY THAT HE'D BEEN CAPTURED?

IT'S TO THE GOVERNMENT'S ADVANTAGE THAT WE THINK HIM DEAD AND NOT CAPTURED...
MOST PEOPLE DON'T TRY TO RESCUE A DEAD MAN!

BUT IF HE'S ALIVE, THEN WE'VE GOT TO RESCUE HIM!

AND WE'VE GOT TO DO IT SOON, BEFORE THEY DON'T NEED HIM ANYMORE!

CHAPTER 17:
A LIGHT IN THE DARKNESS
AT A PRESS CONFERENCE LAST NIGHT, GOVERNOR ALFONSI RESPONDED TO YESTERDAY'S ILLEGAL BROADCAST...

WE WILL NOT REST UNTIL THE TERRORISTS RESPONSIBLE FOR THIS HEINOUS CRIME ARE PUNISHED!

IN THE MEANTIME, THE GOVERNMENT HAS TURNED MARVINS STADIUM INTO A SAFE SPACE FOR ALL THOSE TRAUMATIZED BY THE ATTACK.

IN OTHER NEWS, MARS CONTINUES TO DARKEN WITH THIS GATHERING DUST STORM. OUR WEATHERMAN, SEBASTIAN, HAS MORE...

LIKE ANY MARTIAN DUST STORM, IT'S SPREADING OVER THE PLANET SURFACE, MAKING IT NEAR IMPOSSIBLE FOR SUNLIGHT TO GET THROUGH...

NORMALLY, THIS WOULD LAST ANYWHERE FROM A FEW DAYS TO A COUPLE OF MONTHS, BUT THIS ISN'T YOUR AVERAGE STORM!

WITH INCREASED AIR DENSITY AND WARMER TEMPERATURES, WE NOW HAVE AN ATMOSPHERE CAPABLE OF PRODUCING AN EARTH-LIKE HURRICANE THAT SPANS THE ENTIRE PLANET!

BEST THING IS TO STAY INSIDE OLYMPIA'S BUBBLE AND WAIT THIS STORM OUT.
CAPTAINS BRENDAN AND ERC? THEY USED TO WORK HERE. QUIT LAST NIGHT.

OH? DID THEY SAY WHY?
SOMETHING ABOUT GETTING OUT BEFORE THE STORM HITS.
DID THEY DO SOMETHING WRONG?

Let me know if you hear anything about them.

My card...
Agent Vincent T. Kerr
Department of Martian Security

Sure, you can search their apartment if you want.

But it's like I told you, they cleared out last night.

Any idea where they went?
Nope.

Meanwhile...

I'd have thought it wishful thinking if not for a call I got earlier from one of our contacts in the security sector...

It seems *Firecast* touched at least one heart, and an agent from Kerr's department at that.

Anyway, he told our man that Fr. Mike was taken alive for interrogation, but didn't know where.
Where else?! The prison!

No, he knew that it wasn't in any of the usual places, which makes sense...

If Fr. Mike's supposed to be dead, then any proof to the contrary would hurt the government's credibility.

Sure! They only need him alive long enough to get a few answers. After that, it won't matter *what* happens to his body.
But we've got to get to him first!

Easier said than done! How do you rescue a man when you don't know where he is!?

True enough, but I know someone who might...

Soon...
We need to be very clear on this...

Where we're going has to stay absolutely secret. The lives of many are at stake!
No problem.

Where *are* we going?

To the hospital, or rather, to the Carmelite Convent *under* the hospital.
That's a strange place to put it!

We built the hospital 15 years ago, over the site of the original colonists' chapel.

When the new laws came in, Fr. Mike managed to smuggle the nuns down there by disguising them as nurses.

Here we are.
Brendan and I will get out; the rest of you circle the block a few times until you see us.

We should be back in 10 minutes.

Stay near me!

DING!

DING!

CLACK
CLACK
CLACK
CLACK

DEACON ALEX! WE WERE SO WORRIED ABOUT YOU!

AND WHO'S THIS?
THIS IS MY FRIEND, BRENDAN.
HELLO!

COME IN! CAN I GET YOU ANYTHING?
NO THANK YOU, SISTER. MAY WE SPEAK WITH SISTER JOSEPHINE?
I'LL FIND OUT!

SOON...
I HAD A FEELING HE MIGHT STILL BE ALIVE. IT'S NOT LIKE DAD TO HAVE SOMEONE SHOT IN COLD BLOOD.

PRESUMING FR. MIKE IS STILL ALIVE, DO YOU HAVE ANY IDEA WHERE THEY MIGHT BE KEEPING HIM?

HMM, DAD HAS A SPECIAL PRISON HIDDEN WITHIN THE MEGA MARTIAN ARCADE, MADE ESPECIALLY FOR POLITICAL PRISONERS...
I'D GUESS FR. MIKE ENDED UP THERE.

HOW DO WE GET INTO IT?

There's a door behind the building that leads to the prison.

That's it? What if the door is locked?

Dad always used one 4-digit code back home: 0858...
Maybe it will get you in.

Thank you, Sister, for your help. We should get going. Please keep us in your prayers.
WAIT!

Take some of these!

You're going to need all the help you can get!
1836
1836

Thank you!

Minutes later...
Ha! The Mega Martian! Who would have guessed?!
TAXI

What's that around your neck?

A Miraculous medal. Sister wanted us to have all the help we can get.

Sounds superstitious.

It would be superstitious if we believed it worked by its own power, like a good luck charm...
But it's a *sacramental!*

What? *Another* sacrament??

No, a *sacramental!* You know, like holy water, blessings, rosaries, scapulars...
They're made by the Church to dispose us to receive God's graces.

What's the difference?

Hey! Here's the place. Let's go!
I'll tell you later.

Welcome back to *The Martian Martini*, where today's topic is: Christian terrorism and bad song writing...
ARCADE

We need a plan.

We know where the entrance is and maybe how to get inside, but we'll need a diversion to get that close.

Then what? How are we going to get back out again with Mike?
Huh?

♩ Rum-a-tum-tum ♩ Christians are dumb!
HA ha ha ha ha

I'm good at diversions!
No, let me!

I've, uh, got just the thing for this...
Get in position and I'll make a ruckus in about 20 minutes!

Erc will come with me. Brendan, you go with Ezekiel and get a vehicle that can hold us all.
I remember a fire exit on the east side of the building. We'll meet there in 40 minutes... hopefully with Fr. Mike.

CHAPTER 18:
A FLICKERING FLAME

BEEP
BEEP
BEEP
BEEP

STILL NOT TALKING?? I'M NOT SURPRISED.

I'M FLATTERED THAT YOU'RE WILLING TO GO TO SUCH LENGTHS TO GUARD MY DAUGHTER'S WHEREABOUTS...

BUT A MAN YOUR AGE CAN'T LAST LONG WITH THESE, AH, "MOTIVATION SESSIONS," AND WHAT WILL SHE DO WHEN YOU'RE GONE?

STUBBORN!

WELL, IF YOU DON'T CARE ABOUT YOURSELF, AND YOU DON'T CARE ABOUT MY DAUGHTER, MAYBE YOU'LL CARE ABOUT THIS!

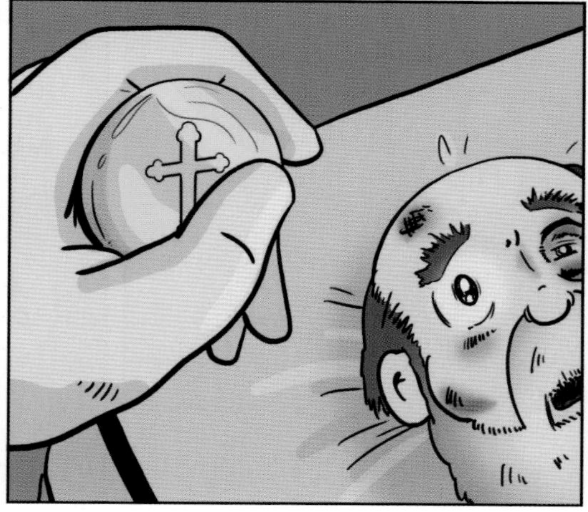

MEANWHILE...

DING!

AH, WE'LL CATCH THE NEXT ONE.

ELSEWHERE...
TELL ME WHAT I WANT TO KNOW, OR I DROP YOUR PRECIOUS BREAD DOWN THE TOILET!

TALK!

WHAT A PITY.

WHAT??

WHAT...
A...
PITY!

WAS IT THAT LONG AGO THAT YOU YEARNED TO RECEIVE JESUS IN YOUR FIRST HOLY COMMUNION?
AND NOW... LOOK AT YOU!

I WAS YOUNG AND STUPID THEN.

REALLY? BACK THEN YOU BELIEVED IN A GOD WHO RULED THE UNIVERSE IN LOVE AND JUSTICE...
NOW YOU THINK YOU DO, EVEN WHILE YOUR PASSIONS RULE YOU!

THEN YOU BELIEVED THAT GOD COULD DO THE IMPOSSIBLE, EVEN CHANGING BREAD AND WINE INTO HIS BODY AND BLOOD...
NOW YOU THINK THERE'S NOTHING YOU CAN'T DO, EVEN BRINGING A DEAD PLANET TO LIFE!

WOULD THAT YOU WERE AS "FOOLISH" NOW AS YOU WERE THEN!

DON'T CHANGE THE SUBJECT! TELL ME WHERE SHE IS!

IF YOU HAD A SHRED OF FAITH LEFT, YOU'D ASK HIM WHO'S IN YOUR HANDS! HE'S THE ONE WHO TOOK HER!

WHAT'S THAT MEAN!?

OUTSIDE...
WE CAN'T JUST STAND HERE. PEOPLE WILL GET SUSPICIOUS.

WHERE ARE WE GOING TO GET A CAR BIG ENOUGH TO HOLD SIX, BUT DISCREET ENOUGH NOT TO RAISE SUSPICIONS?

WE CAN'T CALL A CAB IF WE'VE GOT MIKE WITH US. NOT UNLESS YOU HAVE SOME WAY OF DISGUISING HIM.
SORRY.

IN HOPELESS SITUATIONS, PRAY!

Meanwhile...
Shuffle
Shuffle

There! The back door that Sister told us about!

Did she say anything about a guard?

Let's hope Nathan's diversion does the trick.

Sarah, a nun??

You're lying! My daughter's too smart to waste her life like that.

She's wise enough to know when she's found the Pearl of Great Price that's worth selling everything to buy.*
*Matt 13:46

Well, what do you know!
What?

Frozen Yogurt
There's the answer to our trouble!

Frozen Yog

Frozen yogurt??

EXCUSE ME! HELLO!

HEY, LITTLE MAN! YOU LOOK FAMILIAR.

I FLEW FOR CG INDUSTRIES. WE MET IN OUR CAB SOME TIME AGO...
YOU TOLD ME YOU COULD GET ANYTHING AND EVERYTHING.
OH, YEAH! WATCHA NEED?

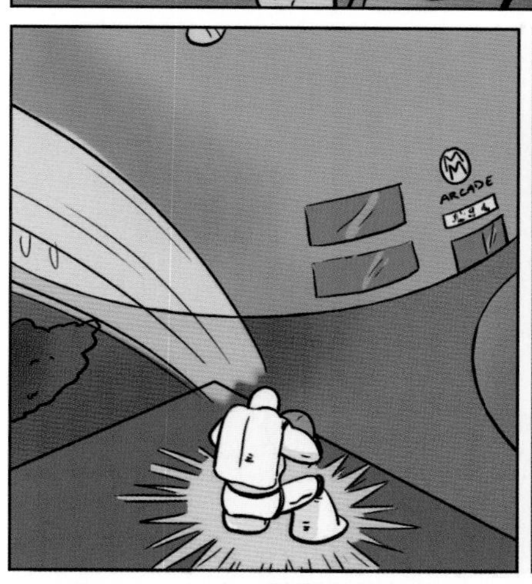
ARCADE

AHEM.

HELLOOO OLYMPIA!

NATHAN?

LISTEN UP IF YOU VALUE YOUR EXISTENCE!

UH, SURE, I CAN GET YOU SOMETHING IN TEN MINUTES. YOU WAIT RIGHT HERE.

HEY, EZEKIEL, GUESS WHAT?

EZEKIEL..?

THAT'S THE SIGNAL! LET'S GO!

WAIT!

SHOOOP

NOW!

Facial Scan
in Progress

IT WORKED!

BEEP!
BEEP!
BEEP!
THUMP

I'LL ASK AGAIN, WHERE IS SHE??
BAM! BAM! BAM!

EH? COME IN!

THIS HAD BETTER BE IMPORTANT.
SIR, IT IS! THE PLANET IS DESTABILIZING!

WHAT ARE YOU TALKING ABOUT??

THE STORM, SIR. IT'S NOT DISSIPATING! THE PLANET CAN'T HANDLE THE HEAT!

WHAT HEAT?? YOU'RE NOT MAKING SENSE!

SIR, IT'S THE SPACE MIRROR. THE PLANET CAN'T HANDLE ITS CONSTANT HEATING. IF IT'S NOT SHUT DOWN, THIS STORM WILL ONLY GET WORSE!

SHUT DOWN THE SPACE MIRROR?? DO YOU HAVE ANY IDEA WHAT WOULD HAPPEN TO THE PARADISE PROJECT WITHOUT IT?!

AS LONG AS THIS STORM GOES ON, SIR, THERE IS NO PARADISE PROJECT!

SHUT IT DOWN, THEN. WE CAN RESTART IT LATER.

BAM!
BAM!
BAM!
AGAIN?? COME IN!

UH, SIR, THERE'S SOME NUT ON THE ROOF NEXT DOOR THREATENING TO BLOW UP OLYMPIA.

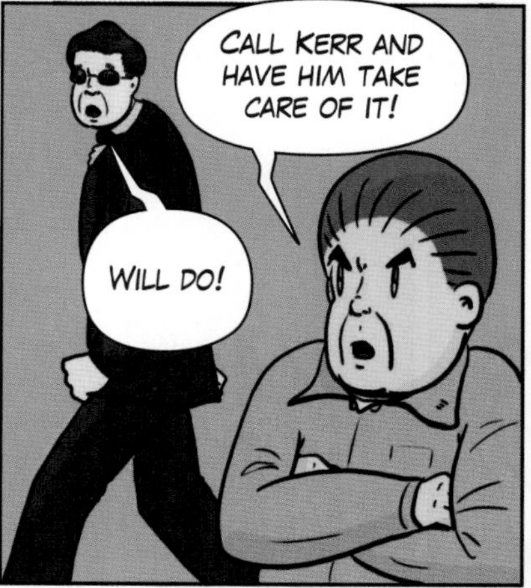
CALL KERR AND HAVE HIM TAKE CARE OF IT!
WILL DO!

IT MUST BE A HUGE BURDEN.

WHAT??

PLAYING GOD. IT'S MORE THAN ANY MAN CAN HANDLE.

YOU'D BE MUCH HAPPIER LIVING IN THE TRUTH.
HMPH! WHAT TRUTH??

That you're just a creature, dependent on the love and mercy of God for every moment of your existence.

Love and mercy of God?? Where is he when everything's falling apart around me!?

There!
LOOK!
Wha...

Luigi.

Remember?

45 years ago...

Jesus, are you *really* in that little piece of bread?

...Oh please, please tell me!

Sigh

Forgive me... forgive me...

Forgive me...

Can he ever forgive me?

SOB
?

Come over here and find out.

CHAPTER 19:
INFERNO
NEWS 7
GO AHEAD AND SHOOT! I'VE PRE-PROGRAMMED THIS SUIT TO LAUNCH THE TF DRONE IF ANYTHING HITS IT!

YOU HEARD RIGHT! I HAVE ONE OF YOUR PRECIOUS VOLCANO-ACTIVATING DRONES!

WHERE'S THE NEAREST VOLCANO, YOU ASK?? WHY, RIGHT UNDER YOUR FEET!!
NOW THAT I HAVE YOUR ATTENTION, THESE ARE MY DEMANDS...

FIRST: FULL, TOTAL, AND UNIMPEDED RELIGIOUS FREEDOM FOR ALL!

SECOND: THE REBUILDING OF ALL DEMOLISHED CHRISTIAN CHURCHES!
SO WHAT DID YOU FIND OUT?

ROBOCO INSISTS THAT NONE OF THEIR TF DRONES ARE MISSING.

FOURTH, A PUBLIC APOLOGY FOR ALL THE LIES AND HARDSHIPS WE'VE SUFFERED!

WELL, WHATEVER IT IS, LET'S ASSUME IT'S DANGEROUS.
GET EVERYONE EVACUATED WITHIN A ONE-MILE RADIUS.

YOU HAVE 20 MINUTES TO GIVE ME YOUR ANSWER!

UH, I THINK I MISSED ONE OF YOUR DEMANDS. CAN YOU START OVER?

SNIPERS, WHERE ARE YOU?

I'VE GOT A PARTIAL SHOT FROM BEHIND.

I'VE GOT A CLEAR VIEW FROM HERE. WAIT...

WHAT'S GOING ON?
THERE'S SOMEONE UP THERE WITH HIM.

NATHAN!

PASTOR! WHAT ARE YOU DOING HERE?? YOU'RE SUPPOSED TO BE GETTING AWAY!

WHAT ARE YOU DOING?? THE PLAN WAS TO MAKE A DIVERSION, NOT A *SCENE!*

FORGET THE PLAN! THIS IS OUR CHANCE TO TAKE BACK OUR RIGHT TO LIVE AS CHRISTIANS!

ALL THOSE YEARS OF SCORN, RIDICULE, EXILE... TODAY WE EVEN THE SCORE!
IF THEY WON'T GIVE US OUR FREEDOM, THEN IT'S TIME WE *TOOK* IT!

THEY ALREADY THINK WE'RE TERRORISTS. ALL YOU'RE DOING IS PROVING THEM RIGHT!
WHAT THEN?! MORE FORGIVENESS?? MORE TURNING THE OTHER CHEEK??
LOT OF GOOD *THAT'S* DONE US!

IT'S TIME WE TRIED A DIFFERENT APPROACH... TIME THEY LEARNED THAT CHRISTIANS CAN **FIGHT BACK!**

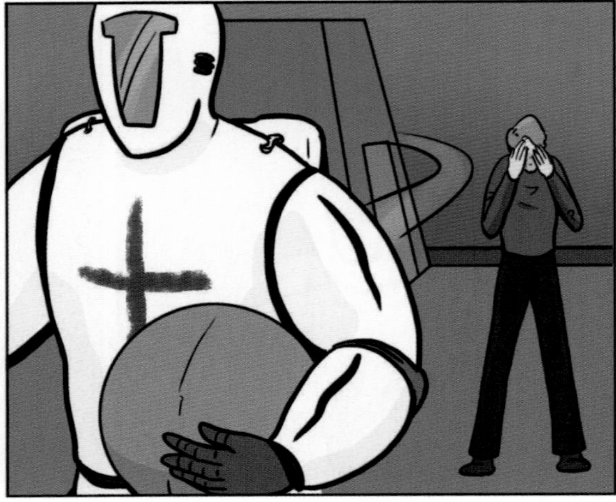

YOU HAVE 20 MINUTES AND NOT A SECOND MORE!

MEANWHILE...

I'M BETTING HE'S THAT WAY.

DO YOU HEAR SOMETHING?

GASP!

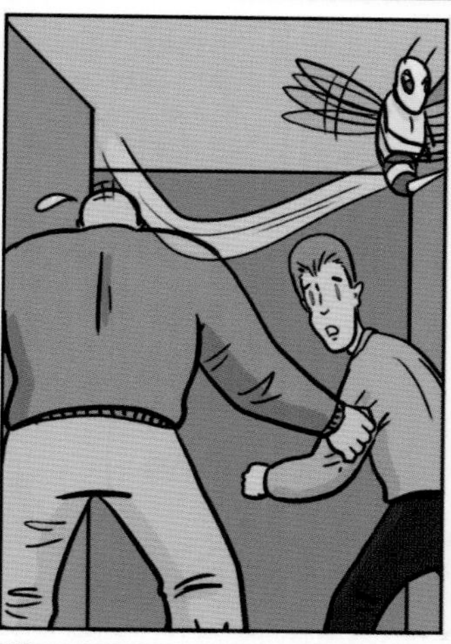

BAM!

DESIST AND RETREAT!

FATHER MIKE'S RESCUERS, I PRESUME?

OUTSIDE...
20 MINUTES, CHRISTIAN?? CAN YOU FIND IT IN YOUR HEART TO GIVE US MORE TIME?
AFTER ALL, ONLY THE GOVERNOR CAN GRANT YOUR REQUESTS, AND WE NEED TIME TO FIND HIM!

YOU'RE DOWN TO 17 MINUTES. BETTER FIND HIM FAST!

OKAY EVERYONE, CLEAR OUT!
HEY! HOW ARE YA?

I GOT YOU A SET OF WHEELS.

ISN'T SHE A BEAUT? THEY DON'T MAKE 'EM LIKE THAT ANYMORE!
ANGELS' BREAD

I'LL TAKE IT.

MEANWHILE...
WHAT'S GOING ON?? WHY ARE YOU HELPING US?

NEVER MIND THAT. TAKE YOUR PRIEST AND GO. THE FARTHER THE BETTER!

LUIGI, DON'T LOSE THE GRACE THAT'S BEEN GIVEN YOU...
DON'T WORRY, FATHER...

THINGS ARE GOING TO CHANGE AROUND HERE.
I PROMISE.

SHOOOP
WHA!

PEACE, OTTO. WHAT'S THE LATEST?

UH, THAT NUT CLAIMS TO HAVE A TF DRONE. KERR THINKS HE'S BLUFFING BUT HAS EVACUATED EVERYONE IN THE AREA JUST TO BE SAFE...
HE THINKS YOU SHOULD LEAVE TOO.

A TF DRONE??

WE USED THEM TO WARM THE PLANET SURFACE BY ACTIVATING VOLCANOS.
IF HE REALLY HAS ONE, THEN WE'D DO BEST TO EVACUATE TO ANOTHER PLANET!

AND, UH, CHRIS CALLED TO TELL YOU THEY CAN'T SHUT DOWN THE MIRROR.
WHY NOT??

NO "OFF" SWITCH? THEY'RE WORKING ON IT.

SIGH
WELL AS LONG AS OLYMPIA'S AIR SHIELD HOLDS WE SHOULD BE SAFE FROM THE STORM FOR A WHILE.

GET THE CAR READY. I'LL BE THERE IN A MINUTE.
YES SIR.

I TRUST YOU HAVE SOME MEANS TO TAKE FATHER AWAY.
YES!

TELL SARAH I LOVE HER AND... THANK HER FOR ALL HER PRAYERS.

FATHER!
SHHH! LET'S GO!

DID YOU FIND SOMETHING TO CARRY US?
WAIT TILL YOU SEE IT!

ANGEL'S BREAD
ANGEL'S BREAD
YOU'VE GOTTA BE KIDDING! THAT!?
IT'S ALL WE'VE GOT.

WHERE'S EZEKIEL?
WHAT ARE WE SUPPOSED TO DO?! STAND IN THE BACK AND WAVE AT KERR AND HIS MEN??

I DON'T KNOW. HE DISAPPEARED A WHILE AGO.
WELL HE CAN'T MISS US IF WE'RE DRIVING *THAT* THING!

LET'S ASSUME HE KNOWS WHAT HE'S DOING AND THAT HE AND NATHAN WILL CATCH UP WITH US LATER.
WHERE ARE WE GOING?
THE HOSPITAL AGAIN. THIS TIME FOR FATHER'S SAKE.

ELS' BREAD
BROOM!

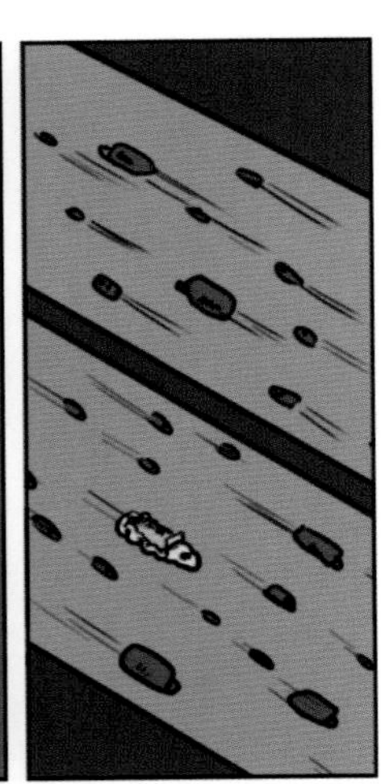

MEANWHILE...
YOU HAVE FIVE MINUTES LEFT! BETTER DECIDE SOON!

IS THE TRAP BOT IN PLACE?
GIVE IT ANOTHER MINUTE.

WE'RE, UH, THINKING ABOUT IT... DON'T GO ANYWHERE!

NATHAN, THESE PEOPLE ARE KILLERS! DO YOU REALLY EXPECT THEM TO PLAY NICE?
I EXPECT THEM TO DO WHAT THEY DO BEST... SAVE THEIR OWN SKINS! THEY EITHER PLAY OR DIE.
IT'S THAT SIMPLE!

THOSE WHO LIVE BY THE SWORD SHALL DIE BY IT. THIS ISN'T RIGHTEOUS IN GOD'S SIGHT!
IT'S THE ONLY WAY! LET WHAT COMES, COME!

TRAP BOT'S READY!

I NEED A DISTRACTION. TAKE OUT HIS FRIEND...

ZAP!
UNGH!

PASTOR...?

NOW!

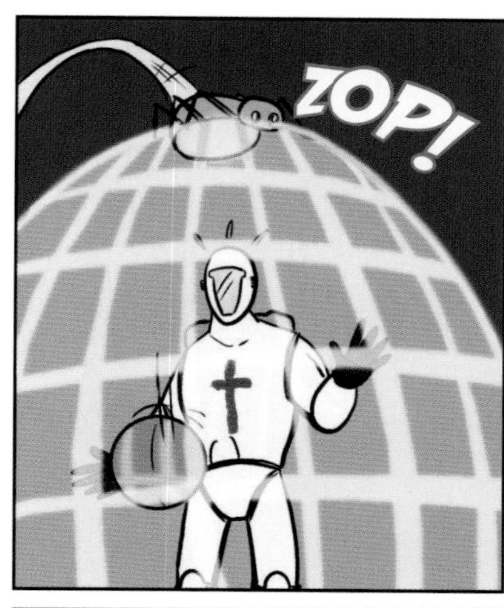
ZOP!
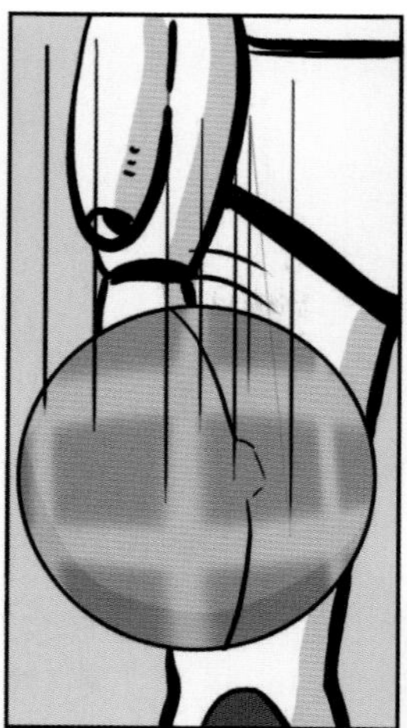

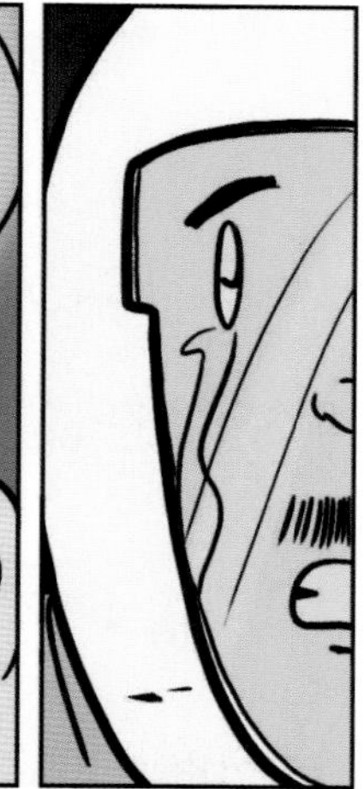

IT IS OUR POLICY NOT TO NEGOTIATE WITH TERRORISTS AND CHRISTIANS!

CLOSE IN ON HIM. HE CAN'T HURT ANYONE INSIDE THAT NET.

BEEP!
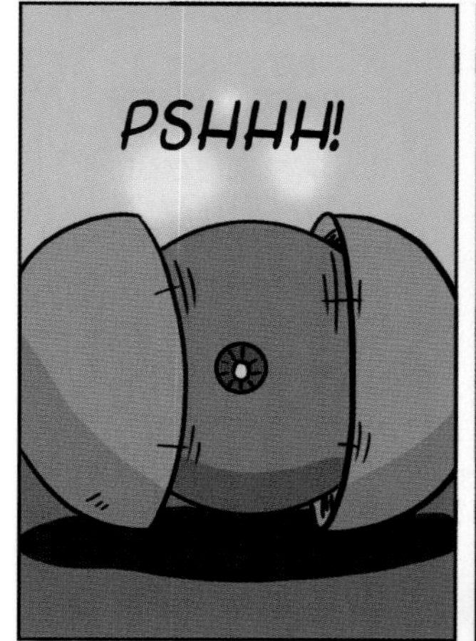
PSHHH!

ACQUIRING...
FSSSSS
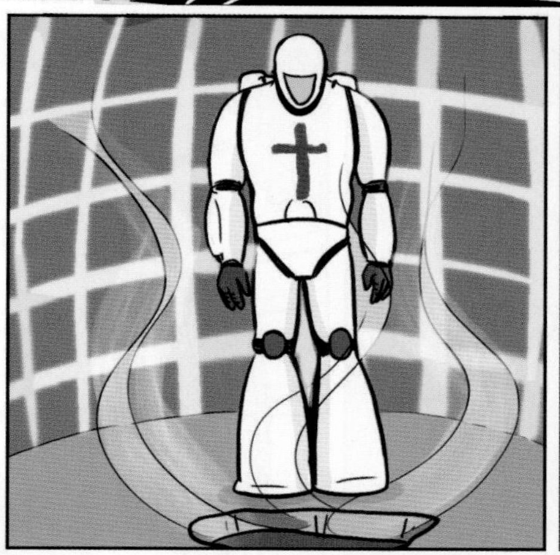

AFTER HIM!

RUMBLE

RUMBLE
UH OH.

CREAK
RUN! RUN!!

CRASH

WE'VE GOT A MAJOR DISASTER HERE. START A FULL-SCALE EVACUATION OF THE CITY.

M9 NEWS

Air quality approaching dangerous levels. Air shield shut down in 15 minutes.
EMERGENC

Air quality approaching dangerous levels. Air shield shut down in 10 minutes.
READ

Looks like everyone's gone.
Not everyone...

Angels' Bread
Do you need help?

No. But this city does.
If the air shield shuts down, the storm outside will fan these fires into an inferno.

What can we do about it?

Erc, shut down that space mirror.
How am I supposed to do that??

Fly up there and destroy it!
But, Father, we don't have a ship!

Erc can use the hospital's space ambulance...
Brendan, I'll need your help.

How am I supposed to destroy a Space Mirror in an ambulance??

SHOOOP
GOD WILL PROVIDE.

I COULD SPOT YOUR GETAWAY CAR FROM A MILE AWAY!

NATHAN...?
WHERE'S EZEKIEL??

THEY KILLED HIM.
BUT I'VE PAID THEM BACK WITH INTEREST!

BOOM

DOES THAT THING SHOOT?
YEAH, WHY?

COME WITH ME! WE'VE GOT A MIRROR TO BREAK!

ERC... BE CAREFUL.

YOU TOO.

SIGH

BRENDAN, THE CAR!

CHAPTER 20:
FIGHTING FIRE WITH FIRE
AMBULANCE
WHO BUILDS A CITY OVER A VOLCANO??

Say a prayer, we're entering the storm!

Whew!

There! What a monster!

EMERG

BOOM

Panis Angelicus Panis angelicus...

ELS' BREAD
Fit panis hominum; Dat panis coelicus...

Figuris terminum; O res mirabilis! Manducat Dominum...

HA! IT'S JUST A BUNCH OF BALLOONS!

ALL RIGHT! I SAW A HATCH BACK THERE TO LET YOU OUT.
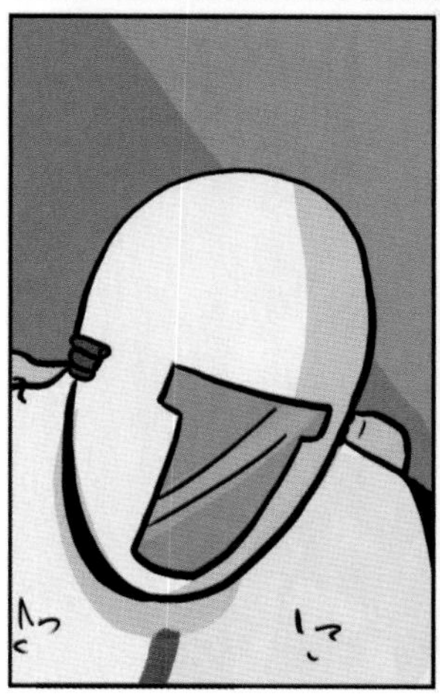

WHAT? GETTING COLD FEET?

I'M NOT THE MAN FOR THIS JOB.

WHAT ARE YOU TALKING ABOUT?? YOU'RE THE ONLY ONE WHO CAN DESTROY THIS THING RIGHT NOW!

THIS NEEDS A HERO NOT A VILLAIN!
SOMEBODY LIKE EZEKIEL SHOULD BE GOING OUT THERE AND SAVING THESE PEOPLE, NOT SOMEONE LIKE ME.

HEY, WE ALL MAKE MISTAKES. HERE'S YOUR CHANCE TO SET THINGS RIGHT.

NO, I CAN NEVER SET THINGS RIGHT...

SOB

SNIFF BUT MAYBE I CAN LESSEN THE DAMAGE.
THAT'S THE SPIRIT!

THIS IS FOR YOU, PASTOR!

POP

MEANWHILE...
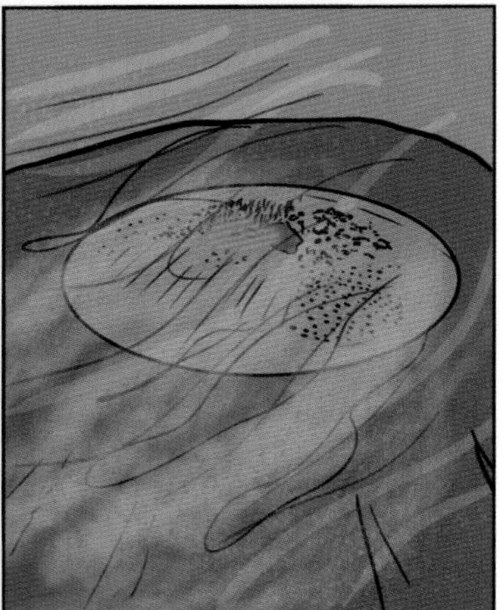

ONLY GOD CAN SAVE US NOW!

THEY DID IT!
THEY DID IT!
WHAT HAPPENED?

HE DID IT!!

NOW TO BRING HIM BACK IN.
VVVRRR

PSSSHHH
HEY, GREAT WOR...

UH OH.

MEANWHILE...

DANGER!
AIR SUPPLY LOW

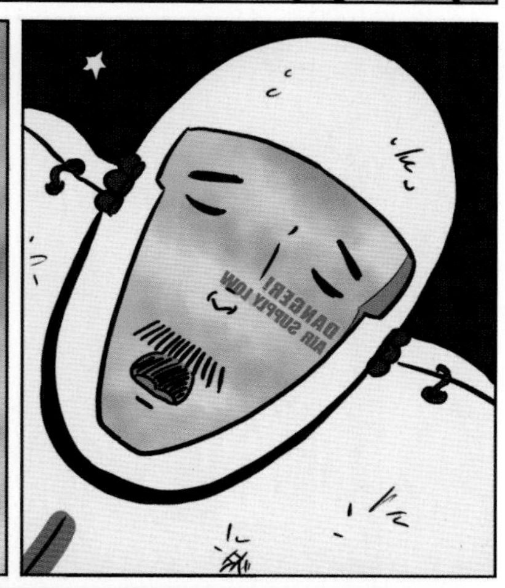

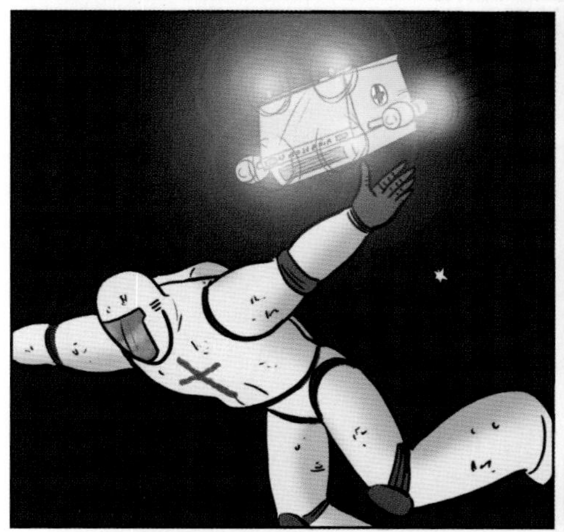

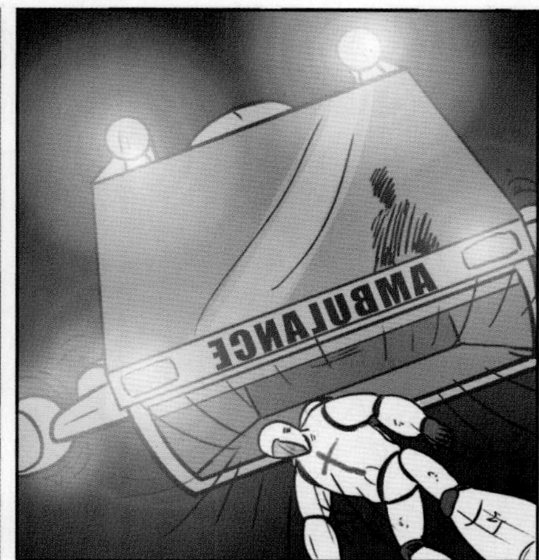
AMBULANCE

SOON...
UGH!
WHY DID YOU SAVE ME?

HEY, MOST PEOPLE WOULD BE GRATEFUL!

I DON'T DESERVE TO LIVE.

WHO DOES??

HEY! LIFE IS A GIFT FROM GOD AND NONE OF US DESERVES IT!

BUT IF HE'S WILLING TO GIVE IT, THE LEAST WE CAN DO IS GLORIFY HIM THROUGH IT...

IT'S NOT TOO LATE.

MEANWHILE...

DID YOU THINK YOU WERE JUST GOING TO WALK RIGHT OUT OF OLYMPIA A FREE MAN?

YOUR WORLD IS GONE. IF NOT FOR GOD'S MERCY, YOU'D BE GONE WITH IT.

I SHOULD HAVE KILLED YOU BACK AT THE HOSPITAL!
WELL, BETTER LATE THAN NEVER!

LEAVE HIM ALONE, KERR!

WHY?? HE'S A CRIMINAL! HE DESERVES TO DIE!

WHAT HE DESERVES, I DON'T KNOW. BUT I KNOW THAT HE'S DONE NOTHING DESERVING DEATH.

WE HAVE A LAW, AND BY IT HE SHOULD DIE!

I MADE THAT LAW AND I CAN UNMAKE IT!

By my authority as governor of Olympia and the greater Martian regions, I revoke the Freedom from Religion laws and pardon all tried under it!

TRAITOR!

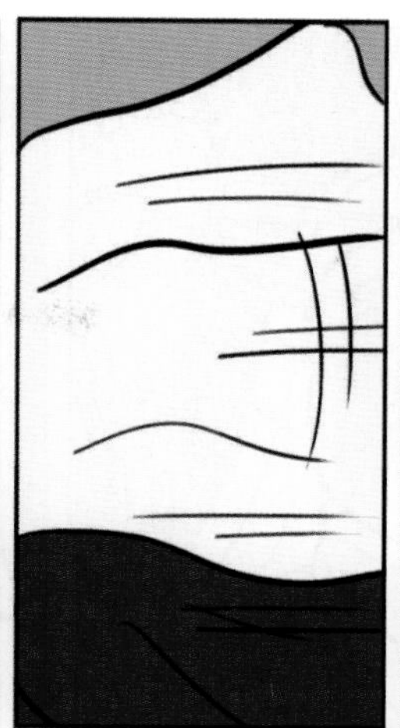

ZAP

NO!

GASP!

ARREST HIM!

SARAH!

SHE'S... SHE'S DEAD...

SOB!

I THINK THERE'S STILL SOME LIFE IN HER.

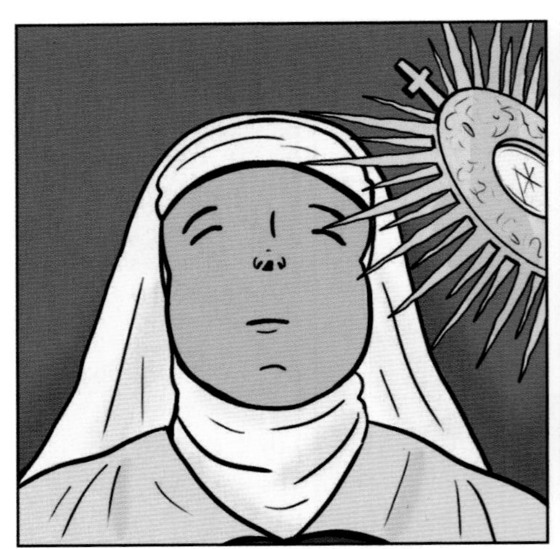
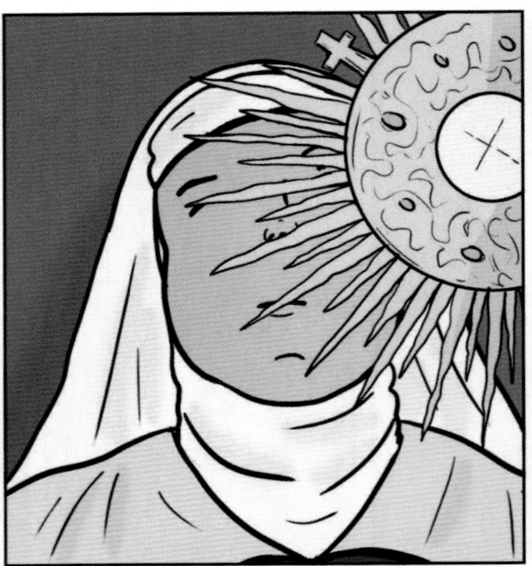
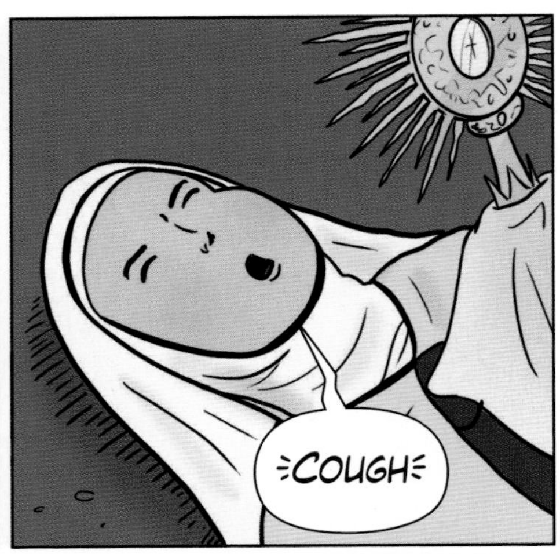
COUGH

SARAH!
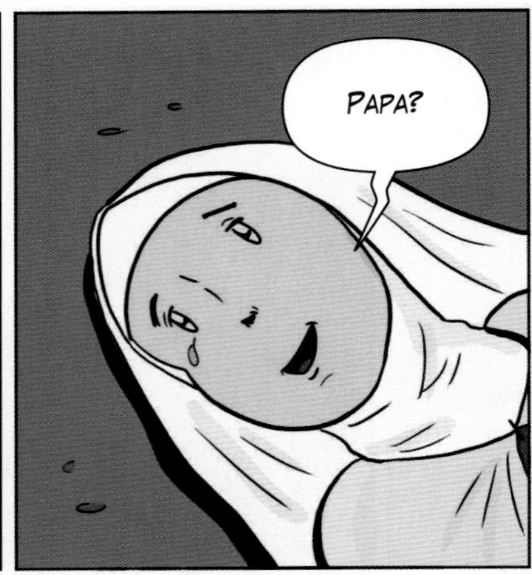
PAPA?

WOOOOSH

WHAT'S GOING ON??
SHE NEEDS HELP!

QUICK! GET HER TO THE EMERGENCY ROOM ON THE MOP!

PROJECT PARADISE PROVED A FAILURE...

BUT AT LEAST ONE WORLD WAS CHANGED!

A FEW MONTHS LATER...
PITY ABOUT THE PARADISE PROJECT. REALLY BURST THE BUBBLE ON A LOT OF PEOPLE'S DREAMS.
EPILOGUE

WE WERE SO CLOSE! WELL, THAT'S HOW THINGS GO.

WHAT BECAME OF THE GOVERNOR AND HIS MEN?

OH, GOVERNOR ALFONSI IS STILL IN CHARGE, BUT HE'S LITTLE MORE THAN A MAYOR NOW.
BETHLEHEM, THE VILLAGE WE BUILT IN THE VALLEY OF MOUNT OLYMPUS, IS A FRACTION OF THE SIZE OF OLYMPIA.

WHY NOT REBUILD OLYMPIA?

THE VOLCANO DESTROYED OUR MAIN WATER SUPPLY. BESIDES, WITH SO MANY PEOPLE LEAVING, IT WAS CHEAPER TO START OVER.

ANYWAY, THE GOVERNOR IS ONE OF THE FEW WHO STAYED ON AFTER THE DISASTER. MOST OF THE OTHER LEADERS LEFT FOR GREENER PASTURES...

SOME, LIKE AGENT KERR, ENDED UP IN JAIL.

WHAT?? THE HEAD OF SECURITY!

YEP. GUILTY OF KILLING AN INNOCENT MAN AND ATTEMPTING TO KILL THE GOVERNOR.

WHAT ABOUT THE GUY WHO ACTIVATED THE VOLCANO? IF ANYONE DESERVES JAIL OR WORSE, IT'S HIM!

Oh, he deserved the very worst! But our governor's a wise man.
When he saw how sorry he was and how useful his skills were, he reduced his sentence to a lifetime of community service.

Besides, I hear he's since gone on to be the new evangelical pastor of Bethlehem and his people love him. Call him their meek and humble shepherd.

I thought religion was banned on Mars!
Used to be...

Now it's thriving, thanks to the governor's benefactions.

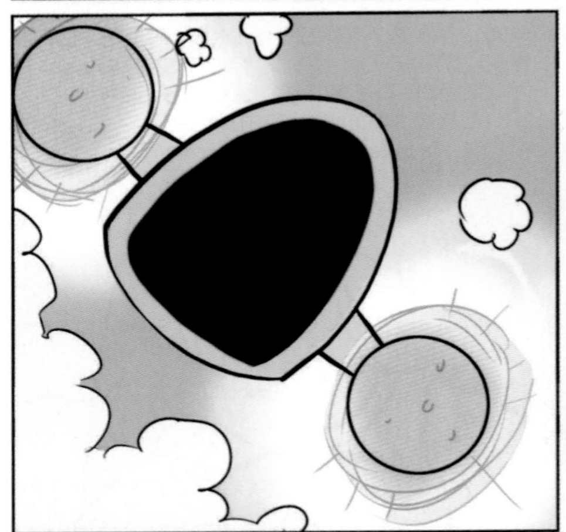

Here we are!

Thanks, Gordan. Any idea where I can find Captains Brendan and Erc?
I hear they're flying for the farmlands these days.

What?
Just ask for a ride to the farms. You'll find them there.

Over the farms...
BOMBS AWAY!!

If half those seeds come up, it'll be a great harvest!
Don't count your wheat before it sprouts!

Hey! There's someone from Earth asking to see you two.
Thanks! We'll be right there!

Captains Brendan and Erc! It's been too long!

Fred! How are you? How's the company?

I'm fine and the company is well. Mr. Givens sends you his greetings.

In fact, he wanted me to talk to you about rejoining our ranks.
Oh?

You may not know it, but Jupiter's moon, Europa, has been flourishing lately...

They're promising to be the next Paradise Planet and people are flocking there in droves!
We need experienced pilots like you out there and soon!

Interested?

Ha ha ha ha ha!

SHOOOP

Was it something I said?

So, what *is* the difference between a sacrament and a sacramental?

THE END

Come to me, all who labor and are heavy laden, and I will give you rest.

PRAYER BEFORE THE BLESSED SACRAMENT

BY ST. ALPHONSUS LIGOURI

MY LORD JESUS CHRIST, WHO BECAUSE OF YOUR LOVE FOR MEN REMAIN NIGHT AND DAY IN THE BLESSED SACRAMENT, FULL OF PITY AND OF LOVE, AWAITING, CALLING AND WELCOMING ALL WHO COME TO VISIT YOU, I BELIEVE THAT YOU ARE PRESENT HERE ON THE ALTAR. I ADORE YOU, AND I THANK YOU FOR ALL THE GRACES YOU HAVE BESTOWED ON ME, ESPECIALLY FOR HAVING GIVEN ME YOURSELF IN THIS SACRAMENT, FOR HAVING GIVEN ME YOUR MOST HOLY MOTHER MARY TO PLEAD FOR ME, AND FOR HAVING CALLED ME TO VISIT YOU IN THIS CHURCH.

I NOW SALUTE YOUR MOST LOVING HEART, AND THAT FOR THREE ENDS: FIRST, IN THANKSGIVING FOR THIS GREAT GIFT; SECONDLY, TO MAKE AMENDS TO YOU FOR ALL THE OUTRAGES COMMITTED AGAINST YOU IN THIS SACRAMENT BY YOUR ENEMIES; THIRDLY, I INTEND BY THIS VISIT TO ADORE YOU IN ALL THE PLACES ON EARTH IN WHICH YOU ARE PRESENT IN THE BLESSED SACRAMENT AND IN WHICH YOU ARE LEAST HONORED AND MOST ABANDONED.

MY JESUS, I LOVE YOU WITH MY WHOLE HEART. I AM VERY SORRY FOR HAVING SO MANY TIMES OFFENDED YOUR INFINITE GOODNESS. WITH THE HELP OF YOUR GRACE, I PURPOSE NEVER TO OFFEND YOU AGAIN. AND NOW, UNWORTHY THOUGH I AM, I CONSECRATE MYSELF TO YOU WITHOUT RESERVE. I RENOUNCE AND GIVE ENTIRELY TO YOU MY WILL, MY AFFECTION, MY DESIRES, AND ALL THAT I POSSESS. FOR THE FUTURE, DISPOSE OF ME AND ALL I HAVE AS YOU PLEASE.

ALL I ASK OF YOU IS YOUR HOLY LOVE, FINAL PERSEVERANCE, AND THAT I MAY CARRY OUT YOUR WILL PERFECTLY. I RECOMMEND TO YOU THE SOULS IN PURGATORY, ESPECIALLY THOSE WHO HAD THE GREATEST DEVOTION TO THE BLESSED SACRAMENT AND TO THE BLESSED VIRGIN MARY. I ALSO RECOMMEND TO YOU ALL POOR SINNERS.

FINALLY, MY DEAR SAVIOUR, I UNITE ALL MY DESIRES WITH THE DESIRES OF YOUR MOST LOVING HEART; AND I OFFER THEM, THUS UNITED, TO THE ETERNAL FATHER, AND BESEECH HIM, IN YOUR NAME AND FOR LOVE OF YOU, TO ACCEPT AND GRANT THEM.

HYMNS TO THE BLESSED SACRAMENT

BY ST. THOMAS AQUINAS

Panis Angelicus

Panis angelicus
fit panis hominum;
Dat panis caelicus
figuris terminum:
O res mirabilis!
manducat Dominum
Pauper, servus, et humilis.
Te trina Deitas
unaque poscimus:
Sic nos tu visita,
sicut te colimus;
Per tuas semitas
duc nos quo tendimus,
Ad lucem quam inhabitas.
Amen.

Bread of Angels,
made the bread of men;
The Bread of heaven
puts an end to all symbols:
A thing wonderful!
The Lord becomes our food:
poor, a servant, and humble.
We beseech Thee,
Godhead One in Three
That Thou wilt visit us,
as we worship Thee,
lead us through Thy ways,
We who wish to reach the light
in which Thou dwellest.
Amen.

Adoro Te Devote

1. Godhead here in hiding,
whom I do adore,
Masked by these bare shadows,
shape and nothing more,
See, Lord, at thy service low lies
here a heart
Lost, all lost in wonder at the
God thou art.

2. Seeing, touching, tasting are
in thee deceived:
How says trusty hearing? that
shall be believed;
What God's Son has told me,
take for truth I do;
Truth himself speaks truly or
there's nothing true.

3. On the cross thy godhead
made no sign to men,
Here thy very manhood steals
from human ken:
Both are my confession, both
are my belief,
And I pray the prayer of the dying
thief.

4. I am not like Thomas, wounds
I cannot see,
But can plainly call thee Lord
and God as he;
Let me to a deeper faith daily
nearer move,
Daily make me harder hope and
dearer love.

5. O thou our reminder of
Christ crucified,
Living Bread, the life of us for
whom he died,
Lend this life to me then: feed
and feast my mind,
There be thou the sweetness man
was meant to find.

6. Bring the tender tale true of
the Pelican;
Bathe me, Jesu Lord, in what
thy bosom ran--
Blood whereof a single drop has
power to win
All the world forgiveness of its
world of sin.

7. Jesu, whom I look at shrouded
here below,
I beseech thee send me what I
thirst for so,
Some day to gaze on thee face to
face in light
And be blest for ever with thy
glory's sight.

Amen.

Suggested Reading

- *Catechism of the Catholic Church*
- *Understanding the Sacraments* by Fr. Peter Stravinskas
- *Sacraments in Scripture* by Tim Gray
- *Where Is That in the Bible?* by Patrick Madrid
- *The Sacraments* by Fr. Matthew Kauth
- *Be Transformed: The Healing Power of the Sacraments* by Bob Schuchts
- *Mysterium Fidei (The Mystery of Faith)* by Pope St. Paul VI
- *The Blessed Sacrament* by Father John A. Hardon, S.J. (Available from Eternal Life Publications)
- *A Key to the Doctrine of the Eucharist* by Dom Anscar Vonier, O.S.B.
- *The Lamb's Supper: The Mass as Heaven on Earth* by Scott Hahn
- *The Bible and the Mass* by Fr. Peter Stravinskas
- *Many are Called: Rediscovering the Glory of the Priesthood* by Scott Hahn
- *The Priest is Not His Own* by Bishop Fulton Sheen
- *Three to Get Married* by Bishop Fulton Sheen
- *A Catholic Handbook for Engaged and Newly Married Couples* by Frederick W. Marks
- *Lord, Have Mercy: The Healing Power of Confession* by Scott Hahn
- *How to Make a Good Confession* by John A. Kane
- *The Spiritual Combat* by Lorenzo Scupoli

ACKNOWLEDGEMENTS

A friend, knowing well the demands of monastic life, once commented that it was a miracle that I ever managed to create these books. I wholeheartedly agreed, especially since these last three years were among the busiest of my life. So, first and foremost, I thank God and all the help that I received from heaven for bringing this book to completion, as well as all the people: friends, relatives, strangers, men and women religious who prayed for me; your prayers (and mine) have been answered! I am deeply grateful for Bishop Gregory Mansour's encouragement and approval, as well as that of my abbot, William J. Driscoll, M.M.A. who made several allowances for me to work on one last book. A big thank you from the bottom of my heart to my brother monks, many of whom took on extra chores and went out of their way so that I might have a little more time to put into finishing the writing and artwork. Nor can I forget the labors of Fr. Robert Nortz, M.M.A. in carefully reading and re-reading each script to make sure it was free from doctrinal errors, as well as Fr. Michael Gilmary Cermak, M.M.A. for giving the whole manuscript a look-over for any heresies that might have crept in when I wasn't looking. Thank you Ben Hatke and my new colorist friend for your invaluable advice in story-telling and artwork. I am always humbled by your generosity! Much thanks to the team at Catholic Answers for their patience and hard work in producing their third-ever graphic novel, especially Todd Aglialoro, Erik Gustafson, and Peggy Stenbeck. Each volume is better than its predecessor! Last, but far from least, thank you to my parents, to Nat & Chris and the kids for their ongoing interest and support. May God bless you ALL in abundance!